A MASKED BALL
AND OTHER STORIES

Other works by A. Craig Bell:

Alexandre Dumas: A Biography & Study

(Translations and Editions of Dumas (Père))
La Route de Varennes
Mes Mémoires (abridged)
En Suisse (abridged)
Histoire de mes Bêtes
Le Vicomte de Bragelonne

ALEXANDRE DUMAS (PÈRE)

A MASKED BALL
AND OTHER STORIES

Translated and with an Introduction by
A. Craig Bell

SUTTON PUBLISHING

Un Bal Masqué (A Masked Ball) first published in 1835
Le Cocher de Cabriolet (The Cabriolet Driver) first published in 1835
Le Curé de Boulogne (The Curé of Boulogne) first published in *Mes Mémoires*, *c.* 1851
Marianna first published in 1859
La Chasse au Chastre (The Elusive Bird) first published in 1841

First published in this edition in 1997 by
Sutton Publishing Limited · Phoenix Mill
Thrupp · Stroud · Gloucestershire · GL5 2BU

British Library Cataloguing in Publication Data
A catalogue record for this book is available from the British Library

ISBN 0 7509 1467 X

Cover detail: Detail from Ball at the Opera *by Edouard Manet, gift of Mrs Horace Havemeyer in memory of her
mother-in-law, Louisine W. Havemeyer,* © *Board of Trustees, National Gallery of Art, Washington, 1873*

 ALAN SUTTON™ and SUTTON™ are the
trade marks of Sutton Publishing Limited

Typeset in 10/11 pt Bembo.
Typesetting and origination by
Sutton Publishing Limited.
Printed in Great Britain by
The Guernsey Press Company Limited,
Guernsey, Channel Islands.

CONTENTS

INTRODUCTION

ALEXANDRE DUMAS was born at Villers-Cotterets in a house then 54 Rue de Lormet, now Rue Alexandre Dumas, on 24 July 1802. His grandparents were the aristocratic Alexandre Davy de la Pailleterie and Marie Cessette Dumas, a Haitian negress. His father was General Alexandre Davy-Dumas, one of Napoleon's brilliant and daring cavalry officers, and his mother Marie-Elizabeth Labouret, daughter of a local tavern-keeper. He was, therefore, technically a quadroon and had frizzy hair and a swarthy complexion, allied with a naïve vanity, amoral instincts, spasms of superstition and the primitive dramatic qualities of genius.

An idle and unscholarly lad, he was the despair of his mother (his father died when Alexandre was only four) and his teachers, hating lessons and much preferring to play truant, exploring the forests of the district and becoming an expert woodsman, snarer and shot. His first attempts at serious reading and authorship were only begun at about the age of sixteen, when the young aristocratic Adolphe de Leuven came into his life. He was the same age as Alexandre, but as polished, artistic and well-educated as young Dumas was raw and ignorant, and, perhaps sensing as yet hidden possibilities, he took him under his wing, giving him classical books to read and lessons in Italian and German. With literary leanings himself, one day he suggested they should collaborate in a vaudeville which he would take to Paris and try to get performed. Though they did this, and in fact wrote more vaudevilles together, it all came to nothing. The young Alexandre, now aged twenty, had at last come to know the joys not only of reading and studying the great classical writers, but the still more potent ones of authorship, all of which made him a changed being.

In 1824 he left his birthplace for Paris full of ambitions, and, thanks to the influence of General Foy, a friend of his father, he obtained a clerkship in the offices of the Duc d'Orléans (later Louis-Philippe). But his clerical work occupied him less than long night-time hours of omnivorous reading and, after seeing some Shakespeare performed by an English touring company, a burning ambition to write plays. This did not prevent him forming a liaison with a Catherine Lebay, who presented him with a son, who was destined to become known to posterity as Alexandre Dumas (fils), the author of many successful plays and above all of the novel *La Dame aux Camélias*. Alexandre's (Père) first play *Christine* (of Sweden), though accepted by the committee of the Théâtre-Français, was shelved until two years later to his bitter disappointment, but he more than made up for this with the next play, again historical, *Henri Trois et sa Cour*. The full study of its inception, performance and success can be read in his *Memoirs*. With it, like Byron with *Childe Harold*, he became famous overnight.

From now on came play after play, success after success, culminating in the then daring *Antony*, a romantic melodrama with a bastard, adulterer and murderer of his mistress as its chief character. This became the first 'modern' play of the era. Dumas went on writing plays almost to the end of his life, and it is as a playwright that he first became famous.

But in 1832 something occurred which was to have significance for the future. A victim of the cholera then raging, and ordered by his doctor to go abroad, he went to Switzerland. On his return he put together from copious notes an account of his travels under the title *Impressions de Voyage: En Suisse*. The work was a huge success – contemporary and later critics alike are agreed that it ranks among the most fascinating of travel books. With its vivid descriptions, drama and humour it is Dumas's first memorable contribution to French literature.

This was followed by a second important revelation – history through the vivid pages of Barante, Froissart and Thierry. His own words in his *Memoirs* depict the effect those historians had on him:

> I perceived a living complete world buried twelve centuries deep in the shadowy abyss of the past . . . I realized for the first time that the past held more than the future, and overwhelmed by my ignorance I pressed my head convulsively between my hands. The study of play writing had taken me several years. How long, then, would the study of history take me?

He lost no time. That study, together with the inspiration of the historical romances of Scott, set him on the road of his true vocation and enduring fame. He wrote: 'It became my ambition to do for France what Scott had done for Britain.' After one or two false starts, in 1838 he wrote his first historical romance *Acté*, set in the time of Nero. It is worth reading, but only just. But then in 1842 came *Le Chevalier d'Harmental*,[1] the first of many to have the true Dumasian verve. After it came the flood – for the next decade there is no parallel in the story of literature. Between 1844 (*annus mirabilis* in which he wrote *Les Trois Mousquetaires*,

---

[1] Better known in English translations as *The Conspirators*.

and began *Monte-Cristo*) and '54 came the Musketeer cycle (*Vingt Ans Après, Le Vicomte de Bragelonne*), the Valois cycle (*La Reine Margot, La Dame de Monsoreau, Les Quarante-Cinq*), the Revolution cycle (*Joseph Balsamo, Le Collier de la Reine, Ange Pitou, La Comtesse de Charny, Le Chevalier de Maison-Rouge*); the whole series ending with the separate *Olympe de Clèves*, set in the reign of Louis XV and one of the finest. With these Dumas accomplished a triple accolade. The sheer verve and élan of the writing were a revelation as to how historical romance could be written and the past recreated, making the similar attempts of Scott and his English successors like Harrison Ainsworth and Lytton seem archaic and stagey. With the Musketeer and Valois cycles and in the characters of d'Artagnan, the three Musketeers themselves and Chicot, the king's jester, he attained the pinnacle of literature's triumphs, namely, the creation of immortal and universal prototypes. Through these characters he made himself the most famed writer of his era. The literary élite and common reader alike came under their spell. *Monte-Cristo* alone brought its author a fortune, and within a few months of publication had been translated into ten languages. Time has not dimmed its lustre. In the critic Maurice Baring's words it might be called with justice 'the most popular novel in the world'.

In all of these he collaborated with Auguste Maquet, and his rôle should be understood. Alone of Dumas's *aides* he was deliberately employed and publicly recognized by Dumas. His name long ago passed from the hierarchy of French literature and is now known only to students of Dumas. Their association began in 1839, when Maquet complained to Dumas that having written a novelette *Le Bonhomme Buvat*, set in the eighteenth century and based on the Cellamare conspiracy, no publisher would accept it. Dumas, always soft-hearted, and interested, took Maquet's manuscript, disappeared for a year to return with Maquet's slim novelette transformed into *Le Chevalier d'Harmental*, his first memorable historical romance. The 'collaboration' continued.

There has been much discussion, in France at least, concerning how much or how little Maquet's share in their work was. The novels written by Maquet after the break with Dumas are forgotten today, while in contrast those written with Dumas are pure Dumas, in W.E. Henley's words, 'one of the greatest masters of the art of narrative in all literature'. The novels, tales, memoirs, books of travel etc. written by Dumas alone meet this same criterion. Who runs may read.

So far Dumas's story has been one of success. But with the advent of the second half of the century the glory began to fade. Following the Revolution of 1848 and the flight of Louis-Philippe, France had become a cauldron of political unrest. This unrest climaxed on 2 December 1851 in the *coup d'état* by which Louis Napoleon, throwing off his sham democracy, made himself Dictator of France. All opposition was stunned and silenced by threat of death. Victor Hugo, disguised as a workman, fled first to Brussels and then to Guernsey. Soon a little French colony had been formed in Brussels. Dumas's fame and glory were now things of the past – his famous château 'Monte-Cristo' was sold at a huge loss,[2] his own Théâtre Historique was shut down and falling into ruin, and like so many of his *confrères* he detested the new regime. Alexandre decided to go to the Belgian capital too, and with only Alexis, his little negro servant for company, began his two-year exile there.

Undeterred, he resumed his customary round of working all hours of the day. But it was as a different author. The calamitous present induced an irresistible nostalgia for the past. Possessed by this, the creator of d'Artagnan, the three Musketeers and Chicot, turning his back on the present, began a series of autobiographical and semi-autobiographical works. He continued first with his *Memoirs* which, though never finished, were to run to ten volumes, and may be said to be one of his most important and fascinating works, re-presenting as it does the great figures and movements of the early part of the century by one of the most vivid pens of that century.

This work in turn served to strengthen his nostalgia. He had written in the *Memoirs*: 'There are impressions which so take hold of us that we try to make them take the same hold on others;' and 'Are there not back there graves of the past which draw me as strongly as the doors of the present? Ghosts who call me with more insistent voices than those of the living?' It was in this mood that he penned the two delightful country novels of his birthplace, *Conscience l'Innocent* and *Catherine Blum*.

His exile came to an end in 1854, and on his return to Paris his first move was to found a journal, *Le Mousquetaire*. For it he continued with his *Memoirs*, finished *La Comtesse de Charny*, wrote *Une Vie d'Artiste* (a biography of Mélingue who had acted in many of his plays, and a minor masterpiece) and began *Les Mohicans de Paris*. He also threw in a host of causeries, dramatic and critical articles crowned by *Mon Odyssée à la Comédie-Française* (a characteristic piece of autobiography) and the *Histoire de mes Bêtes*, narrating with gusto and humour the doings and misdoings of the many and varied pets he housed in his château 'Monte-Cristo'.

But Dumas, the incurable spendthrift, had no idea of finance and management, and despite its initial success the journal had foundered and been given up. This was followed by a second journal, hopefully named *Le Monte-Cristo*. In it appeared *Les Compagnons de Jéhu*, his last notable historical romance; *La Route de Varennes*, a piece of travel-cum-history

[2] Happily the château is now the headquarters of the flourishing Dumas Society.

whereby he traced the flight of Louis XVI and Marie Antoinette from Paris in 1791; *Le Meneur de Loups*, third of the novels of his birthplace and a gripping tale of *diablerie* based on a peasant legend; more characteristic causeries, among which is one recounting in true Dumas style his visit to England to see the Derby.

But yet again, and for the same reasons, the venture failed. Flaubert's notorious novel *Madame Bovary* appeared in 1857, heralding a new type of fiction to be known as Naturalism. As much as fourteen years previously Dumas had written in a preface to his novelette *Herminie*: 'Some day, when we are tired of being a romancer, we will make ourselves a historian and relate certain contemporary happenings so true that no one will believe them.' That day had come. Between 1857 and 1860 he brought out *Black, Madame de Chamblay, Le Fils du Forçat, Le Père la Ruine, L'Ile de Feu* and *Les Mohicans de Paris*. None of these seems to be known to critics or Dumas readers; yet each contains some good Dumas and is worth reading if only for the sake of its astonishing change of aesthetic. No more Romanticism – all is domestic and social, and the characters are one and all everyday contemporary beings. Though unknown and unavailable today, one of them has given posterity a saying, an aphorism, a wisecrack, a reflection – call it what you will – known to all without their awareness of its source. It occurs in the part *roman policier, Les Mohicans de Paris*, that sprawling, shapeless novel of underground Paris which took him four years to write, and in which appears M. Jackal, chief of the Paris police, with his green spectacles, snuff box, and above all with his eternal war cry for every crime – *Cherchez la femme*. From the June of 1858 to the February of 1859 'for a change' he travelled grandly in Russia, where warm greetings, hospitality and homage were meted out to the author of *Les Trois Mousquetaires* and *Monte-Cristo*.

Soon after his return from his Russian travels, now at the age of fifty-seven, he saw the opportunity of realizing a dream of his life, namely a tour of the eastern Mediterranean and the Holy Land. To this end he bought an English-built schooner, *The Emma*, and set sail from Marseilles on 9 May 1860.

But the journey he dreamed of was never undertaken. Unexpectedly there entered into his life Garibaldi, the liberator of Italy. The deeds of the soldier had fired Dumas's imagination, while the historical romances of the writer had gripped the admiration of the soldier. Earlier in the year (1860) Dumas, learning that Garibaldi was in Turin, had gone there specially to meet him. The two became such friends that Garibaldi gave Dumas permission to edit and publish his *Memoirs*,[3] and got from him the

---

[3] These were published in two volumes after appearing as a serial in the *Siècle*.

promise to back his cause and Red Shirts by any available means if and when needed. So now, putting in at Genoa he learned that the Red Shirts had stormed and taken Palermo; and on 28 May came a telegram for him from Garibaldi himself. It was terse but implying much: 'Rally to the sound of my guns.' On receiving it Dumas, true to his promise, knew that his dream voyage was off, and there and then he parted company with his crew, and hastening to join Garibaldi's forces, assisted with both a quantity of arms and his pen. His narration of the campaign from the very battle scenes gives him the accolade of being the first accredited war correspondent.[4]

With the campaign over and won Dumas started on two projects which between them were to keep him in Italy until the spring of 1864, namely, the excavation of Pompeii (Garibaldi had officially appointed him 'Director of Excavations and Museums') and the editing of the journal *L'Indipendente*, devoted to Garibaldi's cause. But on Garibaldi's retirement to his island of Caprera and the anarchy which followed, Dumas, seeing he could be of no further use, left Italy and returned to Paris.

Right up to the year before his death Dumas went on ceaselessly writing; but age was beginning to take its toll. With one notable exception these works lack the verve of his younger days. Among them may be mentioned *La Terreur Prussienne* in which, following the rise of Bismarck and the Battle of Sadowa, he visited the battle sites, then from notes wrote his book, full of ominous foreboding about 'the Prussian menace' and its increasing military threat and danger for his own country. This foreboding was to be realized in 1870 when France was attacked and humiliated.

Les Blancs et les Bleus came next, recounting the main historical events between the execution of Marie Antoinette and the supremacy of Napoleon, and with which he completed his coverage of the whole of French history from the time of Nero to his own day.

Finally came the notable exception, *Parisiens et Provinciaux*, the last of his novels to be published in his lifetime. The fact that it is set partly in Paris and partly in his birthplace helps to account for its charm. The novel deserves to be better known.

The last year of Dumas's life was little more than a prolonging of the end, his physical deterioration taking place with sinister swiftness. He scarcely ever went out or wrote at all, and it became an effort for him to seat himself at his desk. Describing his condition in his biography, *Les dernières Années d'Alexandre Dumas*, Gabriel Ferry wrote:

---

[4] *Les Garibaldiens*. Strangely, the only complete edition of the work is R.S. Garnett's translation as *On Board the 'Emma'* (Benn, 1929) from a recently discovered MS.

Since he was unable to work, no money came in. Distress sat in his hearth and home. He existed from day to day on borrowings from his publisher and advances from his dramatic agent. Even then he did not manage to keep his precarious income for himself: the demands of creditors, or the pitiful tale of some parasite or down-and-out would frequently take from him the greater part of it. On such occasions there would be no money at all in the house, and his cook wondered how he was to cook a dinner for the former lord of Monte-Cristo. When pushed to the last extreme he would send some valuable saved from past opulence to the pawn shop, or a message of desperation would go out to his son. Dumas (fils) never failed help his father out.

In the July of 1870 France declared war on Prussia. The result is history. Defeated and humiliated, the Second Empire fell. Paris itself was invaded. The 'Prussian Terror' of which he had warned his country became a fact. Dumas (fils) seized the opportunity of taking his father away to his new house at Puys, near Dieppe. There in the December his father sank into a coma from which he never recovered, and simply faded out of being. On the very day of the funeral the Prussians took Dieppe.

But Puys was not to have the honour of being his last resting place. Two years later, with the Franco-Prussian war ended, Dumas (fils) had his father's remains exhumed and brought to the place of his birth – the spot he loved above the rest of France. Rightly so. He knew that his father had written of it:

> There my father died, and there I brought my dead mother. There in the charming graveyard, more like a children's flower-decked playground, she sleeps beside the war-worn hero of the Pyramids, the General who fought so well in Egypt. . . . It is there I shall go and sleep in my turn, but as late as possible, please God, for I shall be loth to leave you, dear girl. . . .[5]

His turn had come; and in the spring of 1872 he came for the last time to the woodlands he knew and loved so well, and had made his own.

★ ★ ★

Hidden among the prodigious corpus of his output, these selected tales must seem like a few drops of rain on a vast river; and a reader may well ask how, when and why they came to be written. And the answer to such

[5] From the Preface of his country novel, *Catherine Blum*, dedicated to his daughter, Marie.

a question must be a very nebulous one, since no reference to them can be found in any contemporary sources. All we know of them is the dates of their publication. *A Masked Ball* and *The Cab Driver* were the earliest, and published in 1835 under the title of *Souvenirs d'Antony* only because the publisher believed that any work having reference to the most celebrated play of the time[6] would be sure to sell. The first, with its erotic overtones, is rare among Dumas's writings. Unlike so many French nineteenth-century writers, he had little interest in recounting love scenes. The second shows a touching up of a related incident reminiscent of Dickens's first work, *Sketches by Boz*, and reveals a few facts about himself in the course of it.

The Elusive Bird has a curious history. In 1834 Dumas found himself in Marseilles during his travels in the *Midi*. There he met his old friend Joseph Méry, who over the wine bottles introduced him to a M. Louet, a sportsman who was also a 'cellist in the local theatre orchestra, who, at Méry's urging and Dumas's request, told them the story of his incredible odyssey in stalking a *chastre* (a species of wild pigeon) as far as Italy, where, captured by brigands, he did not return home for twenty years! Louet's narrative lay in the back of Dumas's mind for six years, when, coming to write up his travels as *Le Midi de la France*, he added the story of the famous *chastre* as an epilogue – one so entertaining that it makes the rest seem a little dull, since this impromptu after-dinner yarn is a supreme bravura of story-telling.

The two remaining tales were much later productions. *The Curé of Boulogne* first saw the light as an intercalation in the *Memoirs*. Evidently Dumas thought highly enough of it to include it later still in a collection of sketches called *Bric-à-brac* (1861). This nautical yarn about a simple priest unwillingly absent from his parish for three years shows a lightness of touch and a sense of humour rare in French literature.

Marianna is one of many items published by Dumas on returning from his Russian travels. Although based on a short story by Pushkin and purported by Dumas to have been narrated to him by a Russian friend, the story has the true Dumasian dramatic power.

Although posterity has overlooked these tales, nevertheless they are captivating examples of Dumas's stated wish to express himself in all the multi-varied forms of literature: plays of tragedy and comedy, histories, travel, historical romance, the social novel, the short story – he wrote much of worth in each; and these chips from his workshop are well worth preserving.

A. Craig Bell
1997

[6] *Antony* (1831).

A MASKED BALL

I had said that I was not at home to anybody, but one of my friends insisted on coming in.

My servant announced M. Antony R—— and behind Joseph's livery I caught sight of the skirt of a black greatcoat. It was probable that the wearer of it had for his part seen the flap of my dressing-gown, so it was impossible for me to remain in hiding.

'Very well, let him come in,' said I out loud. 'The devil take him!' was my *sotto voce* comment.

When you are working only the woman you love can disturb you with impunity, because deep down she has always some part in what you are doing.

I, therefore, went to meet him with the half-sulky face of an author who has been intruded on at one of the moments when he hates interruption; but he looked so pale and upset that the first words I said to him were, 'Why, what is the matter with you? Whatever has happened?'

'Give me time to get my breath,' he said, 'and I will tell you all about it. Perhaps it is a dream, or maybe I am mad.' He threw himself into an armchair and let his head drop between his hands.

I surveyed him with astonishment. His hair was wet from the rain, and his boots, his knees and the bottoms of his trousers were covered with mud. I went to the window and saw his cabriolet waiting. I could make nothing of it. Seeing my mystification he said, 'I've been to Père-Lachaise cemetery. Oh, that accursed masked ball!'

I was still completely puzzled, wondering what a masked ball and Père-Lachaise could have to do with one another. As he still did not speak, I began to roll a cigarette in my fingers with all the patience of a Spaniard. When it was ready I offered it to Antony, knowing he usually enjoyed a smoke. He merely gave a nod of thanks, but refused it. Then he suddenly cried out, 'For God's sake, Alexandre, listen to me!'

'But I've been waiting to listen to you for the last quarter of an hour,' I protested, 'and you haven't told me anything.'

'Oh, I'll tell you something, or try to – something extraordinary that has happened to me. You remember the Opera Ball where I last met you?'

'Yes. Well?'

'After leaving you, feeling bored, lonely and depressed, I decided to go to the Variétés, which I had been told was a notorious curiosity to be visited just to see to what depths our society can sink. Oh, why, why, why, did I ever go? I tell you, it must have been fate. I don't know how to describe it to you. I could scarcely believe that what I saw was possible. The place was crowded with men and women masked and dressed up as Pierrots, clowns, women of the streets, God knows what else, all cavorting around like dervishes. I went up one of the staircases, and leaning against a pillar I looked down over this sea of scarcely human beings, all in grotesque dominos, all leaping and thrashing around to the strains of a band which could hardly be heard through their obscene shrieks, yells, laughs and cries. You should have seen them!

'They caught hold of each other by the hands, the arms, the neck. A huge circle was formed, men and women stamping their feet, throwing up above the dim clouds of dust caught by the pale light of the chandeliers, circling at growing speed with obscene posturings, suggestive gestures and cries. Quicker and quicker they circled, swaying backward like drunken men, howling like lost women, delirious rather than joyous, more furious than gratified. They were like a chain-gang of lost souls performing an infernal penance under the lashes of demons. All this din, all this hum, this confusion, this music, were in my head as much as in the hall. I soon came to doubt whether what was before my eyes was dream or reality; I asked myself whether it was not I who was mad and they reasonable. Strange temptations came upon me, to throw myself into the midst of this pandemonium, like Faust visiting the witches' sabbath, and I felt then that I should cry, gesticulate, posture and laugh as they did. Oh, there is only one step from such a state to madness. I was horrified; I flung myself out of the place, pursued to the outer door by howls that were more like the amatory roaring from a den of wild beasts than anything else.

'I paused for an instant under the portico to recover. I did not wish to put myself at risk in the street with my mind in such a tumult, as it still was. I might have stumbled under the wheels of a carriage, not seeing it coming. I was like a drunken man must be when he begins to regain sufficient sense in his fuddled brain to realize his state, and who, feeling his will, though not yet his power, come back, props himself up against a post in the street or a tree in the park.

'At that moment a carriage drew up at the door, and a woman got out, or rather flung herself out of it. She passed under the peristyle, turning her head right and left like a person who is lost. She was clad in a black domino and her face was hidden under a velvet mask. She presented herself at the door.

'"Your ticket?" said the door-keeper.

'"My ticket?" she answered. "I have none."

'"Then get one at the office."

'The domina came back under the peristyle, fumbling madly in all her pockets.

'"No money!" she cried. "Ah, this ring. An entrance ticket for this ring."

'"Impossible," said the woman who was giving out the cards. "We do not do that sort of business." Having said this, she pushed back the brilliant, which fell on the ground and rolled towards me. The domina remained motionless, forgetting the ring, wrapped in thought. I picked it up and handed it to her. I saw through her mask her eyes fix themselves on mine; she looked at me hesitatingly for a moment, then, suddenly putting her arm under mine, "You must get me in," she said, "for pity's sake, you must."

'"I was leaving, Madam," I said.

'"Then give me six francs for this ring and you will have done me a service for which I shall bless you all my life."

'I put the ring back on her finger, went to the office and took two tickets. We went in again together.

'On reaching the corridor I felt her stagger. She clutched my arm. "Are you ill?" I asked.

'"No, it is nothing," she rejoined. "A dizziness, that's all." And she drew me into the hall.

'We re-entered this sordid Bedlam. Three times we went the round of it, forcing our way through the waves of masks, which tumbled and foamed over one another, she wincing at every obscene expression, I blushing to be seen giving my arm to a woman who could listen to such words. Then we came back to the far end of the hall. She sank on to a seat. I remained standing before her, my hand resting on the arm of her chair.

'"Oh, all this must seem very strange to you," she said, "but not more than it does to me, I assure you. I had no idea of it," (she was watching the ball), "for I have never seen such things even in my dreams. But they wrote to me, you see, that he would be here with a woman, and what sort of a woman can it be who would come to such a place?"

'I made a gesture of surprise, which she understood.

'"Yet I am here, am I not, you mean to say? Oh, as for me, that's another matter; I am looking for him, I am his wife. But these people are drawn here by madness and debauchery. But with me, me, it is infernal jealousy. I would have gone anywhere after him; I would have spent the night in a cemetery; I would have gone to the Place de Grève on an execution day. And yet I swear to you that as a girl I never once went out in the street without my mother; as a woman I never stepped out of doors without a footman behind me. But, here I am like all the women who know the way to this place, taking the arm of a man I do not know, and colouring under my mask at the opinion I must be giving him of me. I know all that. Have you ever been jealous, monsieur?"

"'Frightfully," was my answer.

"'Then you can forgive me, for you know it all. You know the voice that cries to you, 'go', as if speaking into the ear of a maniac. You have felt the hand that urges you on to shame and crime, like that of fate. You know that at such a moment one is capable of anything if it will only bring revenge."

'I was going to answer her, but she rose all of a sudden, her eyes fixed on two dominas that were passing before us at that moment.

"'Hush, hush!" she cried, and dragged me along in their wake. I was thrown into the thick of an intrigue about which I understood nothing. I felt all the threads of it beneath my fingers, yet none led me to an end; but this poor woman seemed so upset that she interested me.

'I obeyed like a child, so imperious is a true passion, and we started in pursuit of the two masks, one of whom was clearly a man and the other a woman. They were talking in an undertone and the sounds scarcely reached our ears.

"'It's he," she murmured, "it is his voice; yes, and his figure."

'The taller of the two dominas began to laugh.

"'Yes, yes! it is his laugh," she said; "the letter was true then. Oh God! God!"

'Meanwhile the masks went on and we kept following them; they left the arena and we followed them. They took the staircase leading to the boxes, and we went up after them. They did not stop till they reached the upper tier; we clung to them like their shadows. They entered a small private box, and the door closed upon them.

'The poor creature on my arm frightened me by her agitation. I could not see her face, but pressed against me as she was I could feel her heart beat, her frame shiver, her limbs shake. There was something strange in the way in which I became aware of these unheard-of sufferings, the sight of which was before my eyes, the victim of which I did not know in the least, and the cause of which I knew as little. Yet nothing in the world would have induced me to desert her at such a time.

'When she saw the two masks enter the box and the door close on them she remained motionless for a moment as if thunderstruck. Then she rushed towards the door to listen. Placed as she was the slightest movement might betray her presence and ruin her. I pulled her violently by the arm, unfastened the spring of the adjoining box and drew her into it with me, then, lowering the bars, pulled the door to.

"'If you want to listen," I said, "at least listen from here."

'She fell on one knee and glued her ear to the partition, while I stood erect on the other side, with folded arms and head bent in thought. All that I had been able to see of this woman had seemed to me perfectly beautiful. The lower part of her face, which her mask did not hide, was young and soft and rounded; her lips were red and delicately moulded; her teeth, whose whiteness was set off by the black velvet mask she wore, were small and finely set; her hand was a model for an artist; her waist you could put your fingers around. Her hair, black and silky, escaped in profusion from the hood of her domino, and the little foot which peeped out from her dress seemed scarcely big enough to support her body, light, graceful and airy though it was. Oh, she must be a marvellous creature! Happy the man who should be privileged to hold her in his arms, to see all the faculties of such a soul employed in loving him, to feel her heart on his, palpitating with amorous ecstasy.

'Such were my thoughts when suddenly I saw my companion rise to her feet. Turning to me, she said in a broken and frenzied tone, "Monsieur, I am beautiful, I swear to you; I am young, only nineteen. Up till now I have been pure. Well——" here she threw both her arms round my neck, "Well, I am yours, take me!"

'At the same moment I felt her lips on mine, kissing me wildly, despairingly. Ten minutes later she was in my embrace——

'She came to herself again slowly. I could see through her mask how haggard her eyes were. The lower part of her face was pale, and I could hear her teeth chattering as if in the chill of fever. I can still see it all. She remembered what had taken place and fell at my feet. "If you have any compassion," she said sobbing, "any pity, never look at me again, never seek to know me. Forget everything that has happened between us; I will remember for both of us."

'At these words she rose as quickly as a thought that escapes us, fled to the door, opened it, and turning once more to me cried, "Do not follow me, Monsieur, please do not follow me."

'The door, flung to violently, closed between her and me, hiding her from my gaze. She might have been an apparition. I have not seen her since.

'I have not seen her since, I say, and during the ten months that have passed I have looked for her everywhere: at balls, at theatres, in places of public resort. Every time I saw in the distance a woman with a slender waist, a little foot and black hair, I followed her, I went close to her, I looked her in the face in the hope that her blushes would betray her. But, I never did find her again; I did not see her anywhere but at nights, in my dreams. Ah, then, then she came back; then I felt her; I was conscious of her embraces, her kisses, her caresses, so ardent that there was something infernal in them. Then the mask fell and the strangest countenance appeared to me, sometimes blurred, sometimes clouded, now brilliant as if with an aureole about it, now pale, with the skull white and bare, and eyes in hollow sockets and teeth hideous and sparse. In a word, since that night I have lived consumed with an insane love for a woman I do not know, hoping always and always thwarted in my hopes, jealous without having the right to be so, or knowing of whom I should be jealous, not daring to own such madness, and yet haunted, consumed, devoured by her.'

As he ended these words he drew a letter from his pocket. I took it and read, 'Perhaps you have forgotten a poor woman who has forgotten nothing, who is dying of not being able to forget. When you receive this letter I shall be dead. Go to Père-Lachaise cemetery and tell the lodge-keeper to show you among the recent graves one that will bear on the stone only the name of Marie, and when you find yourself before that grave, kneel down and pray.'

'Well,' Antony continued, 'I got that letter yesterday and went this morning. The lodge-keeper took me to the tomb and I remained there two hours on my knees, praying and crying. Do you understand? She was there! The burning soul had taken its flight; the body, worn out by its emotions, had bent to breaking under the weight of jealousy and remorse. She was there, beneath my feet, and had lived and died a stranger to me! Yes, a stranger, yet assuming in my life such a place as she does in the tomb – a stranger, yet enclosing within my heart as cold and lifeless a corpse as the one that was laid in the grave. Ah, did you ever know such bitter irony! I have lost all hope. I shall never see her again. I could dig up her grave and still not find the lineaments which would enable me to reconstruct her face. And I love her still! Do you realize it, Alexandre? I love her madly. I would kill myself to be with her again – yet she must remain unknown to me for all eternity, as she was in this world!'

At these words he tore the letter from my hand, kissed it again and again and began weeping like a child.

I put my arm around him, and not knowing what to say to comfort him, I wept with him.

THE CABRIOLET DRIVER

I do not know whether, among the readers who may look at these few pages, anyone has ever thought of noting the wide difference that exists between a cabriolet driver and a hackney coachman. The latter, grave, stolid and cold, bearing the outrages of the weather with the calmness of a Stoic, isolated on his box in the midst of society but not of it; allowing himself no distraction but a flick of his whip at a passing comrade; feeling no affection for the two lean nags he drives, no consideration for the victims he conducts; never deigning to exchange so much as a grim smile with them except over the classic words, 'Don't tire your horses, and keep straight on.'

A selfish, callous brute, a surly, lank-haired, foul-mouthed fellow, if ever there was one.

Quite another type of man, your cabriolet driver. You must be in a very bad temper not to relax at the advances he makes you, at the straw he pushes under your feet, at the rug he deprives himself of, whether it rains or hails, to keep you from the rain or the cold; one must be stricken with a very obstinate taciturnity not to answer some of the thousand questions he asks you, or respond to the exclamations which break from him, or the historical facts with which he bombards you.

The fact is that the cabriolet man has seen the world; he has lived in good society; he has driven by the hour a candidate for the Academy, paying his thirty-nine visits – and the candidate's learning has rubbed off on to him; so much for literature. He has carried a Deputy to the Chamber, and the Deputy gave him a veneer of politics. Two medical students got up beside him, they talked of operations, and so he acquired a tinge of surgical science. In short, superficial in everything, but wholly ignorant of very few of the things of this world, he is caustic, witty, talkative, wears a smart cap and always has a relative or a friend who gets him into the theatre for nothing. We are forced to add, to our regret, that the place he occupies is generally a special and conspicuous one in the centre of the pit.

The hackney coachman is a man of primitive times, having no relations with people but those strictly necessary to the exercise of his functions, a knock-me-down man but honourable.

The cabriolet driver is a man of old societies; civilization has touched him, and he has let himself be moulded by it.

Public-house keepers commonly adopt as their sign a hackney coachman with his glazed hat on his head, his blue cloak on his back, his whip in one hand and a purse in the other with the inscription, 'The Honest Coachman'.

I have never seen a public-house sign representing a cabriolet driver under the same moral conditions. No matter! I have a special predilection for such drivers. This may perhaps be due to the fact that I have seldom a purse to leave behind in their vehicle.

When I am not thinking of a drama and so am oblivious, when I am not going to a rehearsal which bores me, or coming back from a play which has sent me to sleep, I talk to them and sometimes get more amusement during the ten minutes drive with them than in the four hours of so-called entertainment from which they are bringing me back.

So then I have a pigeon-hole in my brain devoted solely to these journeys at twenty-five sous.

Among these memories there is one which has left a deep impression on me. Yet it is nearly a year since Cantillon told me the story I am going to tell you.

Cantillon drives Number 221. He is a man of between forty and forty-five, swarthy and with strongly marked features, wearing at the time of which I am speaking, 1 January 1831, a felt hat with the remains of a gold band round it, a top coat of drab cloth, which had evidently once been a livery coat, and boots that had once possessed white leather tops. In the course of eleven months all these remnants of splendour must have vanished. You will understand presently how there comes, or rather, for I have not seen him since the date mentioned, there came to be such a remarkable difference between his garb and that of his colleagues.

It was, as I have said, 1 January 1831, and six o'clock in the morning. I had settled in my head on a series of trips which must be made personally. I had laid down street by street the list of friends whom it is always good to see, especially on New Year's Day; in a word those congenial beings whom one sometimes does not see for six months, whom one advances to meet with open arms and on whom one never leaves a card.

My servant had been to fetch me a carriage; he had chosen Cantillon, and Cantillon believed he had been chosen in preference to others because of his remnants of lace, livery and turn overs. Joseph had scented a former colleague. Besides, his cabriolet was painted chocolate colour instead of being daubed with green or yellow, and, strange to say, there were silver springs which allowed the leather hood to be completely lowered. A smile of satisfaction told Joseph that I was pleased with his sagacity; I gave him leave for the day. I settled myself squarely on excellent cushions. Cantillon drew over my knees a coffee-coloured plaid, gave vent to a click of the tongue, and the horse went off without needing the whip, which throughout our trips remained in the rack, more as an indispensable ornament than a means of coercion.

'Where to, governor?'

'To Charles Nodier's, at the Arsenal.'[1]

Cantillon answered with a nod that meant, 'Not only do I know where that is, but I know the name too.' For my part, I was at that time in the process of writing *Antony*, and as the cabriolet ran very smoothly, I set myself to think over the ending of the third act, which was giving me a lot of trouble.

I do not know of a moment of greater bliss for the writer than when he sees his work coming to fruition. To get there he passes through so many days of labour, so many hours of discouragement, so many moments of doubt. So that when he sees, in this struggle between matter and mind, the idea which he has pressed at all points, attacked on all faces, yielding under his perseverance as a beaten enemy crying for quarter, there is a moment of happiness, proportionate, in his frail organization, to that which God must have experienced when he said to the earth, 'Be!' and the earth was. Like God he can say in his pride, 'I have made something out of nothing, I have brought a world out of chaos.'

True, the world of the dramatist is peopled only by a dozen inhabitants, and fills no larger space in the planetary system than the thirty-four square feet of a stage, and often is born and dies in the same evening.

No matter, my comparison holds none the less – I prefer the one which raises to that which lowers.

I was saying all this to myself, or something like it. I saw, as if behind a veil of gauze, my world taking its place among the literary planets; its denizens spoke as I chose, moved as I pleased. I was satisfied with them, and, coming from a neighbouring sphere, I heard an unequivocal sound of applause which proved that those who examined my world found it to their liking, and I was pleased with myself.

But this did not prevent me from seeing, although the fact failed to rouse me from my trance of pride, that my neighbour was put out by my silence. Uneasy at the fixity of my eyes, shocked at my abstraction, he was making every effort to bring me out of it, now by telling me, 'Governor, the plaid is slipping down,' when without answering I drew it up on my knees again; now by blowing on his fingers, whereupon I silently put my hands in my pockets; and again by whistling *La Parisienne*, whereupon I mechanically beat time. I had told him when I got in that we should be together four or five hours, and he was fairly tormented by the idea that all through that time I should maintain a silence very

---

[1] Charles Nodier (1781–1844), minor French writer. He was librarian at the Bibliothèque de l'Arsenal and a staunch supporter of the Romantic movement.

prejudicial to his willingness to converse. In the end these symptoms of uneasiness increased to a degree which became positively painful. I opened my mouth to speak to him and his face relaxed. Unfortunately for him the idea which I had needed to finish my third act came to me at that moment, and just as I had half turned in his direction, and my mouth was open, I resumed my place calmly and said to myself, 'That's it, that's it!'

Cantillon certainly thought that I had gone quite mad. He heaved a sigh. Then, a moment later he pulled up and said to me, 'Here we are!'

I was at Nodier's door. I should like to talk to you about Nodier, firstly on my own account, seeing that I know and love him, and secondly on yours, who love him, but perhaps do not know him. But that later. For the present my driver is in question. Let us come back to him.

At the end of half-an-hour I came down again; he graciously let down the steps for me. I resumed my place in his conveyance, and after a preliminary 'Brrr!' and some settling down, I found myself back in the sort of easy armchair which had so inclined me to the contemplative life, and said with half-closed eyelids, 'Taylor, Rue de Bondy!'[2]

Cantillon took advantage of my momentary cordiality to say to me rapidly, 'Is not M. Charles Nodier a gentleman who writes books?'

'How the deuce do you know that, eh?'

'I have a novel of his which I got when I was with M. Eugène,' here he sighed, 'about a young girl whose lover is guillotined.'

'*Thérèse Aubert*?'

'That's it! Ah! if I knew him, that gentleman, I could give him a first-rate subject for a yarn.'

'Ah!'

'There's no "ah" about it. If I handled the pen as well as I do the whip, I should not give it to others: I should use it myself.'

'Well, tell me it.'

He looked at me and winked. 'Oh, you, that's not the same thing.'

'Why so?'

'You don't write books.'

'No, but I write plays, and perhaps your story might do for a play.'

He looked at me a second time. 'Was it you who wrote the *Deux Forçats* by any chance?'

'No.'

'Or the *Auberge des Adrets*?'

'No, nor that either.'

'What theatre do you write for, then?'

---

[2] Baron Taylor was an influential committee member of the Comédie-Française and did much to help Dumas to success in his theatrical career.

'So far I have only done them for the Français and the Odéon.'

He screwed up his lips in a manner which gave me clearly to
understand that I had fallen considerably in his estimation. Then he
thought for a moment, and as if making up his mind. 'All the same,' he
said, 'I have been at the Français in my time with M. Eugène. I have seen
M. Talma in *Sylla*. He was just the image of the Emperor. Not a bad
piece, that. And then there was a little bit of an after-piece, with a comic
man in it who wore a footman's coat and made faces. How funny he was,
the scamp, to be sure! All the same, I prefer the *Auberge des Adrets*.'

There was no answer to this. Besides, at that time I was over head and
in theatrical arguments, and had had more than enough.

'So you write tragedies, eh?' said he, giving me a sidelong glance.

'No.'

'What do you write, then?'

'Dramas.'

'Oh, you are a Romanticist. The other day I drove to the Academy a
member who handled 'em finely, these Romanticists. He writes
tragedies, he does; he told me a bit of his last one. I don't know his
name; tall and wizened, and has the Cross and a red tip to his nose. You
must know him, don't you?'

I nodded assent.

'And your story?'

'Oh you see, it is a sad one. A man dies in it.'

The tone of profound feeling in which he said these words increased
my curiosity.

'Tell it all the same,' I insisted.

'"Tell it all the same." That's easily said, and if I cry I shall not be able
to go on.'

I looked at him in my turn.

'You see,' he went on, 'I have not always been a hired coachman, as
you can see by my livery' (here he complacently showed me his facings,
where some fragments of a red bordering were still to be seen.) 'It is ten
years ago that I went into M. Eugène's service. You did not know M.
Eugène?'

'Eugène who?'

'Oh *dame*, "Eugène who?" I never heard him called anything else, and
I never saw either his father or mother. He was a tall young man like you
and about your age. How old are you?'

'Twenty-seven.'

'Just so. Not quite so dark, and then you have hair like a negro and his
was quite smooth, it was. Otherwise a good-looking fellow except that
he was as melancholy, mark you, as a wet blanket. He had ten-thousand
livres a year, but that made no difference, so that for a long time I

thought he suffered from hypochondria. Well, I went into his service. All right. Never any loud talking. "Cantillon, my hat." "Cantillon, put the horse into the cab." "Cantillon, if M. Alfred de Linar comes, tell him I am out." I must tell you he didn't like that M. de Linar. The fact is he was a rip, he was; oh, such a rip! That's it. As he lived in the same hotel with us he was always tumbling over us, enough to sicken you. He came the same day to ask for M. Eugène. I said to him, "Not at home."

'At that moment the other coughed. He heard him right enough. Then he went away, saying, "Your master is an impudent scoundrel!" I kept that to myself, as if nothing had been said. By the by, governor, what number do you want in the Rue de Bondy?'

'Number 64.'

'Here we are, then.'

Taylor was not at home; I merely went in and came out again.

'Well, what next?'

'What next? Oh, in the story. Where are we going first?'

'Rue St Lazare, Number 58.'

'Oh, to Mademoiselle Mars; she's a famous actress, she is! I was saying that the same day we were going to a party in the Rue de la Paix. I got into line. As midnight struck my master came out in a killing humour; he had come across M. Alfred and they had had words. He came back saying, "He is a scoundrel I shall have to chastise."

'I forgot to tell you that my master couldn't half shoot, and handle a sword, too!

'We got to the Pont de la Concorde. There we passed a woman who was sobbing so loudly we could hear her above the rattle of the wheels. My master says to me, "Stop."

'I did so. By the time I turned my head he was out. It was so dark you could hardly see your hand before you. The woman went in front, my master behind. Suddenly she stopped in the middle of the bridge, climbed up and then I heard a splash. My master made no bones about it, but there he was, taking a dive. I must tell you he could swim like a duck.

'I said to myself, "If I stay with the cabriolet, that won't help him much. But as I can't swim, if I jump into the water there will be two to fish out instead of one."

'So I said to the horse – the same nag I have now, but he had four years less on his head then, and two pecks more of oats in his belly – "Stay there, Coco." You would have said he understood me. He stood still all right!

'I took a run and got to the edge of the river. There was a little boat there and I jumped in. It was fastened by a rope; I pulled. I looked for my knife, I had forgotten it; I swore blue blazes. All this time the other was diving like a cormorant. I gave such a hard tug that crack! the rope broke; a little more and I should have tumbled all fours into the river. I pitched over backwards into the boat; luckily I had fallen with the small of my back over a thwart. I says, "It's not the time to stay here counting the stars."

'I spring to my feet, and there the boat was moving. I look for the two oars; in my somersault I had knocked one into the water. I row with the other, I spin round like a top; I say, "I might as well be singing a song for all the good I'm doing. Let's wait a bit!"

'I shall never forget that moment all my life, monsieur. It was frightful. You would have thought the river was made of ink, it was so black. Only from time to time a little wave got up and sent the foam flying. Then in the middle there showed for an instant the girl's white dress, then my master's head as he came up to take breath. Only once did they both come up at the same time. I heard M. Eugène say, "Right, I see her!"

'In two strokes he was at the place where the dress was floating the instant before. Suddenly I saw nothing above water but his legs, which were parted. He brought them together sharply and disappeared. I was ten paces from them, going down the river about the same pace as the current, clutching my oar as if I wanted to crush it, and saying, "Oh Lord, Lord! why can't I swim?"

'An instant later he reappeared. This time he had her by the hair; she was unconscious. It was almost time for my master, too. His chest was rattling and he had only just enough strength to keep above water, for the girl was as heavy as lead. He turned his head to see which bank he was nearest to and saw me.

'"Cantillon," he cried, "help!"

'I was at the edge of the boat, holding out the oar to him, but good Lord, it was more than three feet too short.

'"Help!" he said again.

'I felt furious.

'"Cantillon!"

'A wave passed over his head. I stood there with my mouth open, my eyes fixed on the place. He came up again, and that took a load off my mind. I held out the oar again. He was a bit nearer to me.

'"Courage, master, courage!" I called to him. He could not answer.

'"Let her go," says I, "and save yourself."

'"No, no," says he, "I . . ."

'The water got into his mouth. Ah, monsieur, every hair on my head was wet. I leant out of the boat, holding out the oar. I saw everything spin round me: the bridge, the Hôtel des Gardes, the Tuileries, the whole world; yet I had my eyes fixed only on that head which was sinking little by little, on those eyes level with the water, which were still gazing at me and seemed more than twice the usual size. Then I only saw the hair; the hair sank like the rest. His arm alone was still above water with the fingers clenched. I made a last effort, I stretched out the scull.

'"There you are! Grab hold of it!" I put the oar in his hand. Ah!'

Cantillon wiped his forehead. I breathed hard. He went on:

'People may well say that when you're drowning you would hang to a bar of red-hot iron; he clung to the oar so that he left the mark of his nails in the wood. I rested it against the edge of the boat; that made a see-saw, and M. Eugène came up above the water again. I was shaking so that I was afraid of letting go of the damned oar altogether. I lay down over it, my head on the edge of the boat. I pulled in the oar keeping it down with my body. My master had his head thrown back like a man who had fainted. I kept hauling at the blessed thing, and that brought him a bit nearer. At last I put out my arm and caught him by the wrist; right! I was sure of the business now. I held on to him like a vice. A week later his arm was still black and blue. He had not let go of the little one. I pulled him into the boat and she followed. They lay there at the bottom, the two of them, one not much livelier than the other. I said to my master, "Your servant, sir." I tried to beat the palms of his hands. He had his fingers locked together as if he wanted to crack nuts with 'em. It was enough to give you the creeps.

'I took my oar again and tried to get to the bank. When I have two oars I am no great boatman; with only one it's much the same tale. I wanted to go one way and I turned the other; the current carried me. When I saw finally that I was going down towards Havre I said to myself, "Faith, no mock modesty, let's call for help." And I began to yell like a hyena.

'The chaps in the little cabin where they take the drowned heard me. They put their infernal tub on the water. In a couple of hands' turns they had caught me up. They fastened my boat on to theirs. Five minutes later my master and the girl lay on the floor of the hut side by side like salted herrings.

'They asked me if I had been drowning too. I said, no, but all the same if they would give me a glass of brandy that would put life into me again. My legs were bending like skeins of thread.

'My master was the first to open his eyes. He threw his arms around my neck. I sobbed and cried and wept. My Lord, what a fool a man can be!

'He turned round and saw the young girl whom they were treating. "A thousand francs to you, my friends," says he, "if she does not die. And you, Cantillon, my brave friend, my saviour (I was still crying), bring the cabriolet along."

'You needn't ask if I went off at full tilt. I got to the place where I had left him. There was no cab and no horse, not a bit of it. Next day the police found 'em for us again. Some joker had taken 'em and driven himself home.

'I come back and say, "Nix."

'"All right," he answers, "then fetch a hackney coach."

'"And the girl?" asks I.

'"She has moved the tip of her foot," says he.

'"Splendid!"

'I brought the hackney cab. She had quite come to her senses, only she couldn't speak yet. We carried her to the chaise.

'"Driver, Rue du Bac, Number 31, and sharp's the word."

'I say, governor, here's Number 58, Mlle. Mars.'

'Is your story finished?'

'Finished? Pooh! You haven't heard a quarter of it yet!'

I certainly had to admit that his story was not without interest. I had only one thing to wish our great actress, that she might be as sublime in 1831 as the year before. At the end of ten minutes I was back in the carriage.

'And your story?'

'Where am I to drive you, first?'

'I don't care. Anywhere. Now . . . your story.'

'Ah, the story. We were at "Driver, Rue du Bac, and sharp's the word!"

'On the bridge our young woman lost consciousness once more. My master made me get down on the quay to go and fetch a doctor. When I came back I found Mademoiselle Marie . . . Did I tell you her name was Marie?'

'No.'

'Well, that was her Christian name. I found Mademoiselle Marie had been put to bed with a nurse seeing to her. I can't tell you how pretty she was, with her pale face, her eyes shut, her hands crossed on her breast – she seemed like the virgin whose name she bore, all the more so as it was obvious there was a child on the way.'

'Oh,' said I, 'that was why she threw herself in the river, then.'

'That's just what my master said to the doctor when he told him how it was.

'The doctor made her smell a little bottle; I shan't forget that bottle in a hurry! Fancy! he had laid it on the little table, and, seeing it had made her come round, I thought that it must have been a splendid smell.

'I hung round the table without seeming to want anything, and while their backs were turned, I took out the two stoppers one by one and shoved the mouth of the bottle to my nose. Good Lord! it couldn't have been worse if I'd sniffed in a whole packet of needles.

'"Ah, well! I shall know you another time," I said.

'It had set me crying hot tears. My master said, "Pluck up heart, my friend, the doctor says she will survive."

'Says I to myself, "Well, well! he may be mighty clever, that doctor, but when I am ill, he's not the chap I shall send for."

'In the meantime Mademoiselle Marie had come to her senses again. She looked round the room and said to me, "It's a funny thing, but I don't know where I am. What rooms are these?"

'I said to her, "That may be for the good reason that you've never been here before."

'My master says, "Hush, Cantillon." Then, as he knew how to speak to women, he says to her, "Calm yourself, madam. I shall treat you with all the care and respect of a brother, and as soon as your condition will allow you to be moved to your home, I shall escort you there."

'"I am ill, then?" asked she in astonishment. Then collecting her thoughts, she suddenly exclaimed, "Ah, yes, yes, I remember everything: I wanted——"

'A cry broke from her. "And it is you, sir, who saved me, no doubt. Oh, if you knew what an ill service you did me! What a future of sorrow your devotion on behalf of a stranger has opened before her!"

'I was listening to all this, rubbing my nose which still pricked me. I didn't lose a word, and I'm telling it to you just as it happened. My master consoled her as best he could, but to everything he said she answered, "Oh, if you only knew!"

'Apparently it tried him to hear the same thing over again, for he bent to her ear and said, "I know all."

'"You?" she asked.

'"Yes. You love and have been betrayed, deserted."

'"Yes, betrayed," she replied, "cruelly deserted."

'"Well," said M. Eugène, "confide your troubles to me. It is not curiosity, but the desire to help you that prompts me. It seems to me that I ought to be a stranger to you no longer."

'"Oh, no, no!" said she, "for a man who risked his life as you did should be generous. You, I am sure, have never deserted a poor woman, leaving her no choice but a lasting shame or a speedy death. Yes, yes, I shall tell you all."

'I thought "Good! that ought to be interesting. It begins well, let us listen to the story."

'"But first," she resumed, "let me write to my father, my father for whom I left a farewell letter telling him of my determination, and who thinks I have carried it out. You will let him come here, won't you? Ah! if only in his grief he has not been led into some desperate act! Let me write to him to come at once. I feel that it is only with him that I shall be able to weep, and weeping will do me so much good!"

'"Write, write!" said my master, putting pen and ink near her. "Don't delay an instant. Poor man, how he must be suffering!"

'In the meantime she was scribbling in a pretty little hand like a fly walking. When she had finished she asked for the address of the house.

'"Number 31, Rue du Bac," I told her.

'"31, Rue du Bac!" she repeated with such a start that the inkpot upset over the sheets. After a little while she added with a melancholy air, "Perhaps it is Providence that led me to this house."

'Says I, "Providence or not, it will take a fine lot of spirits of salt to get that stain out."

'My master seemed quite taken aback.

'"I understand your astonishment," she said, "but you are going to know everything. Then you will realize the effect that the address your servant has just given me must have had on me." And she handed him the letter to her father.

'"Cantillon, take this letter."

'I cast my eyes on it. Rue des Fossés-Saint-Victor. "That's a trot for me," says I.

'"Never mind," he answered, "take a cab and be back here in half-an-hour."

'In two steps I was in the street. A cab was passing and I jumped in.

'"Five francs, my friend, to go to Rue des Fossés-Saint-Victor and bring me back here."

'I should like now and again to have such jobs as that, I should.

'We stopped at a small house. I knocked and knocked. The portress came and opened the gate, grumbling.

'"Grumble away!" says I, "but tell me, is M. Dumont in."

'"Oh good Lord!" says she, "do you bring news of his daughter?"

'"Yes, and first-rate news too," I answered.

'"Fifth floor, end of the staircase."

'I went up helter-skelter. A door was ajar; I look in and see an old soldier weeping without saying a word, kissing a letter and loading some pistols. Thinks I, that must be the father, or I am much mistaken.

'I pushed the door. "I come from Mademoiselle Marie," and in I went.

'Then he wheeled round, went as pale as death and says, "My daughter?"

'"Yes, your daughter, Mademoiselle Marie. You are M. Dumont, Captain under the late Emperor?"

'He nodded a yes.

'"Well, here is a letter from Mademoiselle Marie."

'He took it. I am not exaggerating, sir, his hair was standing on end and as much moisture was flowing from his brows as from his eyes.

"'She is alive," cried he, "and it was your master that saved her! Take me to her at once, at once I say! Here, here, my friend."

'He felt in the drawer of a little writing table, took out three or four five-franc pieces and put them in my hand. I took them so as not to humiliate him. I looked at the rooms and said to myself, "You're none too well off, are you!"

'I spun round and slipped the twenty francs behind a bust of the Emperor, and said, "Thank you, Captain."

"'Are you ready?"

"'I am waiting for you."

'Then he began to go down as if he was sliding down the banisters. I said to him, "Listen, listen, old gentleman, I can't see in this snail-shell of a staircase of yours."

'Bah! he was already at the bottom. At last it was all right, we were in the cab. Says I, "With all due respect, Captain, what was it you meant to do with those pistols you were loading?"

'He answered me with a frown, "One was for a villain whom God may forgive but I shall not."

'Thinks I, "Good! that's the father of the child!"

"'The other was for myself."

"'Oh well, it is better that it went off like that," says I.

"'It is not over yet," says he. "But tell me now how your master, that excellent young man, saved my Marie."

'Then I told him all and he sobbed like a child. The sight of an old soldier crying was enough to dissolve stones, so much so that the driver says to him, "Sir, all that is foolishness. I cannot see to drive my horse. If the poor beast had not more sense than we three put together, he would take us straight to the Morgue."

"'To the Morgue!" cries the Captain, shuddering, "To the Morgue! When I think that I had no hope of finding her anywhere but there; that I saw my poor Marie, the child of my heart, laid out on one of those black, slimy, marble slabs! Oh Marie! And there is no danger, is there? The doctor can answer for her?"

"'Don't speak to me about him, that doctor. He's a fine crock."

"'What! then there are still fears for my girl?"

"'No, no, I mean with regard to me and my nose."

'We were getting along all this time, so much so that all of a sudden the driver said to me, "Here we are."

"'Help me, my friend," says the Captain, "my legs won't carry me. Where is it?"

"'There, second floor, where you see light and a shadow behind the curtain."

"'Oh come on, come along!"

'Poor man! he was as white as a sheet. I took his arm under mine. I could hear his heart beating.

"'What if I were to find her dead?" said he, looking at me wildly.

'At the same moment the door of M. Eugène's apartment opened, two flights above us, and we heard a woman's voice crying, "Father, father!"

"'It's her! That's her voice!" says the captain.

'And the old man, who was shaking an instant before, ran up like a young man, went to the room without so much as a "by your leave" to anybody and rushed up to the bedside of his daughter, crying and saying, "Marie! my dear child, my daughter!"

'When I got there it was a picture to see them in one another's arms. The father rubbing the girl's face with his grizzled beard and his old moustache, the nurse weeping, my master weeping, and I weeping quite a heavy shower.

'My master turned to the nurse and me. "We must leave them alone."

'The three of us went out, and he took my hand and said, "Look out for Alfred de Linar. When he comes back from the ball ask him to come and speak to me."

'I went and stood sentry on the staircase and thought, "Your account's settled, or I'm a Dutchman!"

'After a quarter of an hour I heard tinkle, tinkle. It was M. Alfred. He came up the staircase humming. I said to him politely, "Excuse me, but my master would like to have two words with you."

"'Couldn't your master have waited till tomorrow?" he answers jeeringly.

"'It seems not, since he asks for you at once."

"'All right, where is he?"

"'Here I am," says M. Eugène who had heard me. "Will you have the goodness to come into this room?"

'And he pointed to Mademoiselle Marie's. I could not make it out at all. I opened the door. The captain got into a closet, signing me to wait till he was hidden. When it was done, "Come in, gentlemen," says I.

'My master pushes M. Alfred into the room, shoves me out and shuts the door on us. I hear a trembling voice say "Alfred!" and another reply in astonishment, "Marie! you are here!"

"'M. Alfred is the father of the child?" says I to my master.

"'Yes," he answers. "Stay here with me and let us listen."

'At first we heard nothing but Mademoiselle Marie who seemed to be begging something of M. Alfred. This lasted some time. At last we heard a voice saying, "No, Marie, it's impossible. You are mad; I am not my own master about marrying. I belong to a family which would not allow it. But I am rich, and if money . . ."

'There wasn't half a rumpus just then! To save himself the trouble of opening the door of the closet where he had hidden, the Captain just kicked it in. Mademoiselle Marie shrieked, and the Captain let out an oath fit to split the house. Says my master, "Come along in."

'It was high time. Captain Dumont was kneeling on M. Alfred and twisting his neck like a fowl's. My master separated them.

'M. Alfred got up, as pale as death, his eyes fixed and his teeth clenched. He did not cast a glance at Mademoiselle Marie, who had fainted, but came towards my master who waited for him with folded arms.

"'Eugène," he said to him, "I did not know your rooms were a cut-throat den. I shall not come into them again without a pistol in each hand, do you hear?"

"'That is how I hope to see you again," said my master, "for if you came in any other way I should instantly ask you to go out again."

"'Captain," said the other, turning round, "You will not forget that I am in your debt as well?"

"'And you shall pay me on the nail," was the reply.

"'The day is beginning to break," added M. Dumont, "What about weapons?"

"'I have swords and pistols here," said my master.

"'Then have them carried to a cab," said the Captain.

"'In an hour's time, in the Bois de Boulogne, at the Porte Maillot," said Alfred.

"'In an hour's time," answered my master and the Captain together. "Go and find your seconds."

'He went out. Then the Captain bent over the bed of his daughter. M. Eugène wanted to call for help.

"'No, no," said the father, "it is better she should know nothing about it. Marie, dear child, goodbye. If I am killed, M. Eugène, you will avenge me, will you not, and you will not desert the orphan?"

"'I swear it," replied my master. And he threw himself into the poor father's arms.

"'Cantillon, get a cab to the door."

"'Yes, sir. Shall I go with you?"

"'Certainly."

'The Captain kissed his daughter once more, then called the nurse.

"'Now see to her, and if she asks where I am, tell her I am coming back. Come, my young friend, let us be off."

'They went into Eugène's room. When I came back with the coach they were waiting for me downstairs. The Captain had pistols in his pockets; M. Eugène had swords under his cloak.

"'Driver, to the Bois de Boulogne."

"'If I am killed," said the Captain, "you, my friend, will give this to my poor Marie. It is her mother's wedding ring. A worthy woman, young man, who is now with God. Then give orders for me to be buried with my Cross and my sword. I have no other friend but you, or other relative than my daughter. So you and she will follow my coffin, and that's all."

"'Why these thoughts, Captain? They are very gloomy for an old soldier."

'The Captain smiled sadly.

"'Everything has gone badly with me since 1815, M. Eugène. Since you have promised to watch over my girl, better a young and rich protector than an old and poor father."

'He ended and the other dared say no more, and the old man remained silent as far as the place of meeting. A hackney coach followed us a few yards behind. M. Alfred got out of it with his seconds. One of them came up to us.

"'What arms has the Captain chosen?"

"'Pistols," answered he.

"'Remain in the coach and look after the swords," says my master.

'Then they all five plunged into the wood. Ten minutes had scarcely passed when I heard the report of two pistols. I started as if I had not expected it. There was an end of one of them, for ten minutes more went by without the sound being repeated. I had thrown myself on the back seat of the coach not daring to look. Suddenly the door opened.

"'Cantillon, those swords," said my master. I handed them to him. He held out his hand to take them, and on his finger was the Captain's ring.

"'And – and . . . Mademoiselle Marie's father?"

"'Dead."

"'Then the swords?"

"'Are for me."

"'For heaven's sake, let me come with you."

"'Come if you like."

'I jumped out of the vehicle. My heart was as small as a grain of mustard and all my limbs shook. My master entered the wood and I followed. We had not gone ten yards when I caught sight of M. Alfred erect and smiling between his seconds.

"'Take care," said my master, pushing me aside. I jumped back. I had all but trodden on the Captain's body.

'M. Eugène gave one glance at the corpse and then went forward to the group, let the swords fall on the ground and said, "Gentlemen, see if they are of the same length."

"'You do not want to put the matter off till tomorrow then?" said one of the seconds.

"'Impossible!"

"'Oh, my friends, don't distress yourselves," said M. Alfred, "the first tussle has not tired me. Only I should be glad of a glass of water."

"'Cantillon, go and fetch a glass of water for the gentleman," says my master. I felt as much inclined to obey as to go and hang myself. My master signed to me again, and I went off towards the restaurant at the entrance to the Bois. We were scarcely one-hundred yards from it. In two shakes I was back again. I handed him the glass of water, saying to myself, "There! And may it poison you!" He took it; his hand did not shake, only when he gave me back the glass I saw that he had so gripped it between his teeth that he had taken a piece out of the edge.

'I turned round, throwing it away over my shoulder, and saw that my master had got ready during my absence. He had only kept his shirt and trousers on, and the shirt sleeves were turned up to the top of the arm. I went to him.

"'Have you no orders to give me?" I asked.

"'No," answered he. "I have neither father nor mother. If I die" (and he wrote a few words in pencil) "you will give this paper to Marie."

'He gave another look at the Captain's body, then went towards his opponent, saying "Come, gentlemen."

"'But you have no second," objected M. Alfred.

"'One of yours will act for me."

"'Ernest, go over to this gentleman's side."

'One of the two crossed over accordingly. The other took the swords, placed the men at four paces from one another, put the hilt of a sword in the hand of each, crossed the blades and fell back, saying, "Now, gentlemen."

'Instantly both of them took a step forward, and their blades were engaged up to the hilt.

"'Step back," says my master.

"'I am not in the habit of disengaging," answered the other.

"'Very well." And he stepped back a pace, and stood on his guard again.

'Their blades wound round each other like snakes at play. M. Alfred was the only one to attack. My master, keeping his eye on the sword, was ready with his parry and as cool as in a fencing saloon. I was in a fine rage. If the other man's servant had been there, I should have strangled him.

'The fight still went on. M. Alfred laughed bitterly, my master was calm and cold.

"'Ah!" came from M. Alfred. His sword had touched my master on the arm and the blood was flowing.

"'It is nothing," he said. "Carry on."

'I wasn't half sweating, I can tell you!

'The seconds came forward, but my master motioned to them to retire. His opponent took advantage of the movement and lunged. My master

was just too late with his parry, and the blood flowed from his thigh. I sat
down on the grass. I could stand no longer.

'Nevertheless M. Eugène was as calm and cool as ever, only his parted
lips showed his teeth clenched. The moisture was running from his
opponent's brow; he was growing weaker.

'My master made a pace forward and the other disengaged.

'"I thought you never disengaged," said the former.

'M. Alfred made a feint and my master parried so strongly that his
opponent's blade went aside as if he were saluting. For a moment his
breast was uncovered, and my master's sword was buried in it up to the
hilt.

'He flung out his arms, let fall his foil and only kept his feet because
the sword held him up by spitting him. My master drew out his blade,
and he fell.

'"Have I behaved like a man of honour?" he asked of the seconds.

'They made a gesture of assent and came forward to M. Alfred.

'My master returned to me.

'"Get back to Paris and fetch a notary to my house, to be there on my
return."

'"If it is to make M. Alfred's will," says I, "it is scarcely worthwhile,
seeing that he is writhing like an eel and spitting blood, which is a bad
sign."

'"It is not for that," said he.'

'What was it for, then?' I asked.

'To marry the girl,' replied Cantillon, 'and acknowledge her child.'

'He did that, did he?'

'Yes, sir, and finely. Then he says to me, "Cantillon, my wife and I are
going to travel, but you understand it would only distress her to see you.
Here's a thousand francs; I'll give you my cabriolet and horse to do what
you like with. And if you want anything, mind you apply to me and no
one else."

'As I had the stock-in-trade I became a driver. There's my story,
governor. Where shall I drive you to?'

'Home; I'll finish off my calls another day.'

So I went home and wrote down Cantillon's story just as he had told it
me.

THE CURÉ OF BOULOGNE

Here is a little story very popular in the French Navy, and I should like to pass it on and to see it adopted to the same degree by landlubbers – tell me if you don't think it well worth relating.

* * *

On 14 November 1766, an open carriage, drawn by post-horses, containing three naval officers, one on the front seat and the other two on the back one – which signified a decided difference in their rank – was driving along the Bois de Boulogne, coming from the Barrière de l'Etoile and going towards the Avenue de Saint-Cloud. By the Château de la Muette it passed a priest who was walking slowly along one of the pavements reading his breviary.

'Hi! postillion!' shouted the officer sitting at the front of the carriage, 'stop a moment, please.'

The postillion stopped. This request, given in a loud voice, and the noise made by the postillion in pulling up his horses, naturally made the priest raise his head and fix his eyes on the carriage and its three occupants.

'*Pardieu*! I am not mistaken,' said the officer. 'It is really you, my dear Remy!'

The priest gazed in astonishment. Gradually, however, his face cleared as light dawned on him, and his expression turned from amazement to smiles.

'Ah,' he said at length, 'it is you!'

'Yes, it is I, Antoine de Bougainville.'

'Good heavens! What have you been doing with yourself during the twenty-five years since we parted?'

'What have I been doing with myself, dear friend?' repeated Bougainville. 'Come and sit down by me a few minutes and I will tell you.'

'But . . . .' The priest looked round him uneasily, as though he were afraid to go far away from his home. Bougainville understood his fear.

'Don't be anxious; we'll go quite slowly' he replied.

A valet got down from the seat behind and lowered the step. 'It is a quarter past eleven,' said the priest, 'and Marianne expects me for dinner at twelve.'

'In the first place, where do you live? But sit down, sit down.'

He lightly drew the priest by his gown, and the priest sat down.

'Where do I live?' asked the latter.

'Yes.'

'At Boulogne . . . I am curé of Boulogne.'

'Ah! ah! My congratulations! You always had the vocation.'

'So, you see, I entered Orders.'

'Are you satisfied?'

'Enchanted. The benefice of Boulogne is not one of the best – it has only an income of eight-hundred livres; but my tastes are modest, and there still remain four-hundred livres over to give away to the poor.'

'Good old Remy! . . . You can go at a slow trot, so that we shall lose as little time as possible.'

The postillion set the horses to the required pace, which, moderate though it was, none the less brought a cloud of distress on the curé's countenance.

'Set your mind at rest,' said Bougainville. 'We are going in the direction of Boulogne.'

'You see,' the Abbé Remy said laughing, 'I have been curé of Boulogne for twenty years; Marianne has been with me fifteen years, and never, except when detained by the side of a dying parishioner, have I been five minutes later than twelve; punctually at twelve the soup is on the table, and . . . you understand?'

'Yes; don't be afraid, I do not want to upset Marianne. You shall be home by twelve exactly.'

'Very good. Now my mind is easy. But talk about yourself a little. So you are wearing the uniform of the Navy?'

'Yes; I am captain of a ship.'

'How is that? I thought you were a barrister.'

'I thought so too, my dear Remy! But after a couple of years at it I came to dislike it. You see, I have always loved action, and the sea, and the thought of passing the rest of my life in chambers and being involved in petty quarrels frightened me. Then by chance a friend of mine, high up in the Navy and to whom I told my woes, said, "Why don't you throw it up and join us? It's a healthy life, and full of action – just what you need." After thinking it over I took his advice. Thanks to his influence and, if I may say so, my determination to get on, I worked my way up and eventually ended up becoming captain of a ship.

'In 1756 I went as captain of dragoons with the Marquis de Montcalm, charged with the defence of Canada——'

'Splendid! splendid!' interrupted the Abbé Remy. 'I can just see you doing it! Go on, go on!'

The abbé, completely fascinated by Bougainville's narrative, had not noticed that the horses had quietly passed from a slow to a quick trot. Bougainville continued his story.

'In Canada I was pretty much master of my future; I had only to conduct myself well to attain to anything. I was put in charge of several expeditions by the Marquis de Montcalm, which I brought off successfully.

'For instance, after a march of sixty leagues through forests which were believed to be impenetrable, sometimes over tracts of country covered with snow, sometimes on the ice of the River Richelieu, I advanced as far as the end of the Lake of Saint-Sacrement, where I burned an English flotilla under the very fort which protected it.'

'What!' said the abbé, 'was it you who did that? Why, I read the account of that event; but I did not know you were the hero . . .'

'Didn't you recognize my name?'

'I knew the name but not the man. . . . How could you expect I should recognize in a member of the Basoche, whom I left studying law and aspiring to become a barrister, a dashing fellow who burns fleets in the far-away depths of Canada? . . . you can surely see that it was impossible!'

At this moment the carriage stopped before a posting-house, 'Oh!' said the Abbé Remy, 'where are we, Antoine?'

'We are at Sèvres, old fellow.'

'At Sèvres! What time is it?'

Bougainville looked at his watch.

'It is ten to twelve.'

'Oh! Mon Dieu!' exclaimed the abbé, 'but I shall never be at Boulogne by noon.'

'That is more than probable.'

'A league to go!'

'A league and a half.'

'If only I could find a posting-carriage——'

He rose to his feet in the carriage and cast a look round him as far as his sight could reach, but there was no sign of any sort of vehicle.

'Never mind,' he said, 'I will walk.'

'You shall not walk!' said Bougainville.

'What! you will not let me walk?'

'No, it shall not be said that you caught pleurisy because you took a drive with a friend.'

'I will go quietly.'

'Oh, I know you! You would be afraid of being scolded by Mademoiselle Marianne, you would hurry, arrive in a state of perspiration, drink cold water and give yourself inflammation of the lungs. . . . Some idiot of a doctor would purge you instead of bleeding, or bleed you instead of purging; and three days later, goodbye, there would be the end to the Abbé Remy!'

'All the same, I must return to Boulogne . . . Hi! postillion! postillion! Stop!——'

The carriage, with its fresh horses, set off at a quick trot.

'Listen,' says Bougainville, 'this is the best thing to do——'

'The best thing to do, my good friend, my dear Antoine, is to stop the horses, so that I can get down and make my way back to Boulogne.'

'No,' says Bougainville, 'the best thing to be done is for you to come with me as far as Versailles.'

'As far as Versailles?——'

'Yes; as you have missed Mademoiselle Marianne's dinner you must dine with me at Versailles. While I am receiving final commands from His Majesty, one of these gentlemen will undertake to find a travelling carriage to convey you back to Boulogne.'

'Of course that would be a great pleasure, but——'

'But what?'

The abbé felt in his pockets, plunging both hands in up to the elbows.

'But,' he continued, 'Marianne has not put any money in my pockets.'

'Never mind about that, my dear Remy! At Versailles I will ask the king for a hundred crowns for the poor of Boulogne; the king will grant them me, and I will give them to you. You can borrow a few crowns from them until you return in the travelling carriage to Boulogne, and the thing is settled.'

'What! You think the king would give you a hundred crowns for my poor?'

'I am sure of it.'

'On your word of honour?'

'On my faith as a gentleman!'

'Oh! that decides me, then.'

'Thanks! You would not come for my sake, but you will for the poor. It seems to be more worthwhile being one of your poor parishioners than your friend!'

'I do not say so, my dear Antoine; but you know, a curé who deserts his post must have a good reason.'

'An excuse? . . . Oh! if you slept away, I do not say . . .'

'What! if I slept away!' exclaimed the Abbé Remy, terrified. 'Do you mean, then, to make me stop away the night? . . . Postillion! Hi! postillion!'

'No, don't be afraid. . . . At the rate we are going we shall reach Versailles in an hour; we shall dine by two, and you can leave at three.'

'Why at three, and not at two?'

'Because I must have time to see the king and ask him for the hundred crowns.'

'Ah! that's true.'

'Three hours for you to return by carriage from Versailles to Boulogne; you will be home at six o'clock.'

'What will Marianne say?'

'Bah! when she sees you return with a hundred crowns given to you by the king, Marianne will be happy and proud of your influence.'

'Upon my word you are right. . . . You must tell me all the king says to you; this adventure will give her enough to talk of to her neighbours for a week.'

'So it is settled; we are to dine at Versailles?'

'Agreed as to Versailles! But now tell me the end of your story.'

'Ah! true. . . . We had got to my expedition on the Saint-Sacrement. It earned me the rank of quarter master of one of the Army Corps, and the commission to go to Versailles to explain the precarious situation of the Governor of Canada, and to ask for reinforcements for him. I stayed two and a half years in France without obtaining anything I asked for. True, I got what I did not ask for, that is to say, the Cross of Saint-Louis and the rank of colonel in the staff of the regiment of Rovergne. I arrived in Canada just in time to receive from the Marquis de Montcalm the command of the Grenadiers and Volunteers, at the famous retreat from Quebec, which I was ordered to effect. When Montcalm arrived beneath the walls of the town he thought he might risk a battle. The two generals were killed: Montcalm in our ranks; Wolfe in those of the English. Montcalm dead, our army defeated, there was no means of defending Canada. I returned to France, and went through the campaign of 1761 in England, as aide-de-camp to M. de Choiseul-Stainville.'

'Then it was you to whom the king made the present of two guns?' interrupted the curé.

'Who told you that?'

'I read about it in the *Gazette de la Cour* . . . how could I have dreamt this Bougainville was my friend Antoine?'

'What did you think of the present?'

'Bah! I thought it well deserved . . . but, all the same, I thought the king ought to have given this M. Bougainville, whom I was far from suspecting was you, something more easily carried about than two cannon; for, of course, though a great honour, one cannot carry them about wherever one goes.'

'There is truth in what you say,' Bougainville resumed, laughing, 'but, as simultaneously the king made me captain of a ship, and entrusted me with the founding of a settlement for myself and the inhabitants of St Malo, in the Malouines, I thought my two cannon might be of use there.'

'Ah! quite right,' said the Abbé Remy; 'excuse my ignorance of geography, my dear Antoine, but where are the Malouines?'

'I beg your pardon,' said Bougainville, 'I should have called them the Falkland Isles, for it was I who gave them their name of the Malouine Isles in honour of the town of St Malo.'

'Very good!' said the abbé, smiling, 'I recognize them under that name! The Falkland Isles belong to the archipelago of the Atlantic Ocean; I know where they are, near the southern extremity of South America, to the east of Magellan Straits.'

'Upon my word,' said Bougainville, 'Strong, who christened them, could not have determined their bearing more accurately himself. You study geography, then, in your benefice of Boulogne?'

'Oh, when I was young I always longed to go as a missionary to the Indies . . . I was born with the love of travel, and I would have given anything to go round the world . . . in those days, but not now.'

'Yes, I understand,' said Bougainville, 'but today it would put you out of your regular habits. So you have never travelled?'

'My friend, I have never been further than Versailles.'

'Then you have not been on the sea.'

'No.'

'You have never seen a ship?'

'I have seen a few sails at Auxerre.'

'That is something, but it can only give you a very poor idea of a frigate of sixty guns.'

'So I should imagine,' added the abbé innocently. 'So you say you went to the Malouine Isles, where the Government had authorized you to found a settlement. I have no doubt that you did so?'

'Unluckily the Spaniards, after the peace of Paris, laid claim to these islands; their claim was considered just by the Court of France, which gave them up on condition they indemnified me for the money I had laid out.'

'But did they?'

'Yes, my dear friend, they gave me a million francs!'

'A million francs? *Peste*! what a pretty sum.' It will be observed that the good abbé nearly swore! 'Now,' he continued, 'where are you going?'

'To Havre.'

'What to do? Forgive me, perhaps I am inquisitive.'

'Inquisitive? Oh, certainly not! . . . I am going to Havre to see a frigate of which the king has made me captain.'

'What is its name?'

'*La Boudeuse*.'

'Is it a very fine ship?'

'Superb!'

The abbé heaved a sigh. It was evident the poor priest thought what pleasure it would have given him in times past, when he had been free, to look at the sea and to go over a frigate.

This sigh led to a fresh interchange of looks and smiles between Bougainville and the two officers. Both smiles and glances passed unnoticed by the worthy abbé, who had fallen into so profound a reverie that he did not come to until the carriage stopped before a large hotel.

'Ah! so we have arrived,' he said. 'I am very hungry!'

'Good! We will not have to wait as the dinner was ordered beforehand.'

'What a delightful life a sea captain's must be!' said the abbé. 'He gets millions from the Spaniards; he travels post in a good carriage; and, when he arrives, he finds a dinner all ready for him! Poor Marianne, she will have had to dine without me!'

'Bah!' said Bougainville, 'once does not mean always. We will dine without her, and I hope her absence will not take away your appetite.'

'Oh, don't be anxious . . . I am really very hungry.'

'Well then, to table! to table!'

'To table!' merrily repeated the abbé.

It was a good dinner; Bougainville was a gourmet; he drank no other wine than champagne; the fashion of icing it had just been invented.

All priests, whether they be curés of a small town or hamlet, or officiating priests of a chapel without a congregation, are inclined to pamper their stomachs; the Abbé Remy, modest though he was, had the sensual side with which nature had endowed the palate of the ecclesiastic. At first he would not drink more than a few drops of wine in his water; then he mixed wine and water in equal parts; then, finally, he decided to drink his wine pure. When Bougainville saw he had arrived at this point he rose and announced that it was time for him to present himself before the king, to whom he was going to address the request relating to the poor of Boulogne. In the meantime the two officers were to keep the abbé company. As Bougainville had said, he was absent for about an hour. In spite of the assurances of the officers the worthy priest's hopes seesawed up and down in a way which did credit to his kindliness of heart.

'Well!' he said, when Bougainville returned, 'what about my poor people?'

'It is not three-hundred livres the king has given me for them,' said Bougainville, drawing a roll from his pocket, 'but fifty louis!'

'What! fifty louis?' exclaimed the Abbé Remy, quite overcome by this regal bounty, 'one-thousand two-hundred livres!'

'One-thousand two-hundred livres.'

'Impossible!'

'Here they are.'

The abbé held out his hand.

'But the king has given them on one condition.'

'What?'

'That you drink to his health.'

'Oh, if that is all!'

He held out his glass, into which Bougainville tipped the neck of the bottle.

'Stop! stop!' said the abbé.

'Come, now!' Bougainville insisted, 'half a glass? The king would not be pleased to see only half a glass drunk to his health.'

'Really,' the abbé said jovially, 'one-thousand two-hundred livres deserve a whole glass. Fill it quite full, Antoine, and here's to the king's health!'

'To the king!' repeated Bougainville.

'Ah!' said the abbé, putting his glass on the table, 'this is what one might call a real orgy! True, it is the first I have taken part in, and I shall not have the opportunity of a second for a very long time.'

'I tell you what——' said Bougainville, resting his elbows on the table.

'Well?' replied the abbé, whose eyes were shining like carbuncles.

'Something you ought to do.'

'What is it?'

'You tell me you have never seen the sea.'

'Never.'

'Well, you ought to come to Havre with me.'

'I . . . come to Havre with you? . . . But you are not dreaming of such a thing as that, Antoine?'

'On the contrary, it is just what I am doing. Have a glass of champagne.'

'Thanks, but I have already drunk too much.'

'Ah! to the health of your poor people . . . that is a toast you cannot resist.'

'Very well, but only a drop, mind.'

'A drop! When you drank the glass full to the king? Ah! that is not scriptural, my dear Remy. The Scripture says, "The first shall be last . . ." A full glass for the poor of Boulogne, or none at all.'

'Here goes, then, for a full glass; but it is the last.'

The abbé, good Catholic as he was, emptied his toast to the poor as gaily as that to the king.

'There!' said Bougainville. 'Now it is agreed we set off for Havre.'

'Antoine, you must be mad!'

'You shall see the sea, old friend . . . and such a sea! Not a lake like the poor Mediterranean, but the ocean, which rolls round the world!'

'Stop tempting me, you dreadful fellow!'

'You yourself admit it has been the desire of your life to see the ocean!'

'*Vade retro, Satanas!*'

'It is only a matter of a week.'

'A week! Good heavens, if I absent myself for a week without leave I shall lose my benefice!'

'I have foreseen that, and as monseigneur, the Bishop of Versailles, was with the king, I got him to sign you a permit, telling him you were coming with me.'

'You told him that?'

'Yes.'

'And he signed me a permit?'

'Here it is.'

'Dear me! It is indeed his signature, I would swear to it.'

'My old friend, you are a sailor at heart.'

'Give me my fifty louis and let me go.'

'Here they are, but you shall not go.'

'Why not?'

'Because I am authorized by the king to hand you fifty more at Havre, and you will not be so mean a Christian as to deprive your poor people – your children, the flock over which the Lord has given you charge – of fifty beautiful golden louis!'

'Very well!' cried the abbé, 'then I will go to Havre! But it is only for their sakes I consent.'

Then, stopping suddenly, 'No,' he said violently, 'it is impossible!'

'Why impossible?'

'Marianne!——'

'You shall write to her to relieve her anxiety.'

'But what shall I tell her?'

'Tell her that you have met the Bishop of Versailles, and that he has given you leave to go to Havre.'

'That would be lying!'

'To lie for a good motive is not a sin, but a virtue.'

'She will not believe me.'

'You can show her the permit signed by the bishop.'

'Yes, that is true . . . Ah! you barristers, you soldiers and sailors, you stop at nothing.'

'All you want is pen, ink and paper.'

The abbé reflected for a minute, and no doubt with sad misgivings wrote a few lines of explanation to his Marianne. Bougainville took it and dispatched it to the post by a personal messenger; then he said, 'Now, forward for Havre!'

Some two hours later they entered the port. The sight of the sea, the real sea, and the various vessels gladdened the abbé's innocent heart. One particular ship, riding gracefully in the roadstead, held his eye.

'Oh!' asked the abbé, 'what is that magnificent vessel?'

'My friend,' said Bougainville, 'that is *La Boudeuse*, where we are expected for dinner.'

'What! Do you mean me to go on board?'

'Surely! You would not come all the way to Havre and return without having seen over a ship! Why, my dear friend, it is just as though you went to Rome without seeing the pope.'

'True enough,' said the abbé, 'but when shall we return?'

'When you like . . . after dinner – it is for you to decide. You shall give your orders and be captain on my vessel.'

'Very good! Let us set off, then . . . we have taken fourteen hours to come, but I shall take quite five or six days to return.'

'What does it matter? you have leave for a week.'

'I know that quite well, but you see, there is Marianne——'

'Picture in your mind the cries of joy she will utter when she sees you again.'

'Do you think they will be cries of joy?'

'Zounds! I hope so indeed!'

'I hope so too,' said the abbé in tones expressive more of doubt than hope.

Then, like a man who has flung his cap over the windmill, 'Come, come,' he said, 'to the frigate!'

Bougainville appeared to be waited on by genii, who also did the bidding of the abbé, and to such good purpose that when the latter exclaimed, 'To Havre!', he found the carriage all ready; and in the same way, when he exclaimed, 'To the frigate!', he found the captain's gig waiting. He got into the boat and sat down by Bougainville, who took the helm. A dozen sailors waited with raised oars.

Bougainville made a sign; the twelve oars fell and hit the water with so regular a movement that they seemed to strike it as one man. The boat flew over the sea like those long-legged spiders which glide over water. In less than ten minutes they were alongside. It hardly need be said that the maritime wonder called a frigate roused the enthusiasm of the good abbé to the highest pitch; he asked Bougainville the name of each mast, of each yard and of each rope. No sails were set, but they were hanging in brails. In the middle of the naming of the different parts of the ship, a messenger came to tell the captain that dinner was served. The abbé and he went down into the captain's cabin. This cabin might have vied with any drawing-room belonging to one of the richest châteaux around Paris in comfort and elegance. The abbé's surprise increased more and more. Fortunately, although it was November, the sea was all ablaze; it was one of those beautiful autumn days which seem like a farewell sent to the earth by the summer sun before its disappearance for six long months.

The abbé was not in the least seasick, a fact which caused the superior officers who were admitted to the captain's table, and the captain himself, to offer their congratulations. However, towards the middle of dinner it seemed to him as though the motion of the frigate was increasing; Bougainville replied that it was the ebb tide, and delivered a learned lecture on tides. The abbé listened to his friend's scientific dissertation with the greatest animation and attention; and, as he was not unacquainted with physical science, he made observations in his turn which seemed to call forth the delighted admiration of the officers.

The dinner carried on longer than the diners themselves realized; nothing is so ignorant of the passing of time as interesting conversation, enlivened with good wine. Then came coffee, that sweet nectar for which the abbé confessed a weakness. Captain Bougainville's coffee was such a delectable mixture of Mocha and Martinique, that, between delicate sips betraying the connoisseur, the abbé declared he had never tasted its equal. Then, after the coffee came liqueurs, those famous liqueurs de Madame Anfoux which were the delight of the gourmets of the latter part of the last century. Finally, when the liqueurs had been enjoyed, and the abbé proposed to go back on deck, Bougainville raised no opposition to this desire; but he was obliged to give his arm to his friend up the companion-way, the abbé naïvely attributing his instability of balance to the champagne, Mocha coffee and liqueurs de Madame Anfoux which he had drunk.

The frigate was on the larboard tack, with her head to the north-east, and the wind blowing free; all sail was set, including lower and top-gallant studding sails. Only the stay-sails were stowed. They must have been making a good eleven knots.

The abbé's first feeling was that of whole-hearted admiration for this masterpiece of naval architecture in full sail. Then he noticed that the frigate was moving. Next he looked around him – and, finally, he uttered a cry of terror. The land of France looked no more than a cloud upon the horizon. He regarded Bougainville with an expression in which was concentrated all the reproaches of a betrayed confidence.

'My dear fellow,' said Bougainville, 'it gave me so much pleasure to see you, my oldest and dearest comrade, that I resolved we would remain together as long as possible. I wanted a chaplain on board my frigate; I asked His Majesty to let you fill this post, and he graciously granted it, together with a stipend of a thousand crowns. Here is your commission.'

The abbé flung a frightened glance at the signed commission.

'But,' he said, 'where are we going?'

'Round the world, my dear fellow!'

'How long does it take to go round the world?'

'Oh, from three to three and a half years, more or less——'

The abbé fell back, overcome, against the raised stand of the officer's watch.

'Oh!' he murmured, 'I shall never dare to appear before Marianne again!——'

'I promise to take you to the presbytery and to make your peace with her,' said Bougainville.

On 15 May 1770, the frigate *Boudeuse* re-entered the port of St Malo. It was exactly three and a half years since she had left Havre; Bougainville was not a day out in his calculation. In that time she had been all round the world.

Heaven alone knows what passed at the first meeting between the Abbé Remy and Marianne!

MARIANNA

FOREWORD

We were at Petrosky Park, staying at the house of my old friend, Dmitry Paulovitch Nariskin, and I had just transcribed the last lines of Youkovsky's account of Pushkin's dying hours. I wondered at the strange fatality which had brought to a similar untimely end the lives of the two great Russian poets, Pushkin and Lermontoff – the one killed by Dantès, the other by Martinoff, both in the prime of life and the fullness of their talent, when, having already given the world so much, they promised still more.

'Why these duels with pistols, that unchivalric weapon, the weapon with which the coward who quakes and trembles will sometimes kill his adversary just because he trembles, while the man with heart of steel and steady hand misses because his hand and heart are firm and steady?' I demanded.

'Because we never wish to fight except seriously, so we do not fight except for serious matters,' replied Prince K.

'Well and good,' I replied, 'but do you really think that all duels, in Russia, even the most disastrous in their result, have a serious cause? Don't you know that among your young officers, inactive and unoccupied in out-of-the-way garrison towns, some reach such a pitch of utter boredom as to fight purely and simply as a diversion, with just the same readiness with which we fight, or rather used to fight, in France, till first blood was spilt for any stupid wager, for a bottle of champagne?'

With this I turned to appeal to Monsieur Panovsky, a highly distinguished litterateur of whose kindness of heart I had had more than one opportunity of judging.

'You are quite right,' he said, 'and I could relate to you half a score of anecdotes in support of what you say.'

'One will be enough, my dear sir; will you tell me one?' I asked him. 'This journey which I am taking has its philosophic side, too, although so far as I can, I conceal that aspect under the veil of the picturesque. Well, I should be glad to have an account of a duel in which the gravity of the result made a startling contrast with the futility of the cause.'

'That falls just right,' said he. 'It so happens I have a diary in my hands at this moment, with full permission to do what I please with it. It includes among other matter a series of letters from a retired Captain of Hussars. I am having extracts from these letters printed. Tomorrow I will send you the proofs, you can have the stuff translated, and your wish will be gratified.'

The conversation then turned to other things. Next morning, faithful to his promise, Monsieur Panovsky, to whom I here tender my very best thanks, sent me the following narrative.

A.D.

CHAPTER I

A MESS BREAKFAST

Our regiment happened to find itself in May 18— in a dirty little village in the governorship of Valins, where, in the middle of the most dilapidated 'isbas' (these 'isbas' belong to Jews) is to be found a charming manor house, with a large garden, and round about it a number of small houses belonging to what is called the factorship of the estate. These houses were occupied, some by the factor or steward and the chief dependants of the owner; others by government employees, to whom they were let. Some of these employees, and indeed some of these dependants, with or without the permission of the proprietors, were in the habit of sub-letting these houses at exorbitant rents to our officers. They themselves retired to the dirty 'isbas' of which I have spoken, and which the Jews – who, themselves, slept goodness knows where, under the sheds, with the fowls and the crows, or in the stables with the horses and cows – gave up to them in turn at the highest price they could manage to extract.

The village is situated on the summit of a fairly high conical hill in the middle of a wide plain, which surrounds it on all sides, broken by the meanderings of a small river, and studded with clumps of sombre green fir.

It is as though it were built on an island, the coasts of which are beaten by rolling waves of golden grain in the months of July and August. On the distant horizon, facing the mansion of which I have spoken, can be discerned a long dark line – the frontier forests of Austria.

On the left, the plain extends for several miles, and here and there, like flights of birds which have alighted and are warming themselves in the sun, are to be seen groups of houses forming small straggling villages, each one of which has its name, unknown ten leagues off. On the right rises a mountain which commands the whole plain, and even the hill on which is built the village whose situation I have just described. It is covered with wood to the summit; it is called 'The Holy Mountain' because, according to local legend, on its summit was built the first Christian chapel which existed in the country at the time of the persecutions of the early Christians.

Finally, on the side facing the entrance to the manor house, neither towns nor villages are to be seen, but only vast meadows and a water-mill by the side of the river, which feeds two ponds fringed by silver-leaved aspens, leaves that are for ever moving, even when no breath of wind stirs the foliage of the other trees.

At half a verst from these ponds tower two pyramids, situated at about eighty feet from one another, called 'The Tombs of the Two Brothers'. The inhabitants of the district relate that they are so named because, as a matter of fact, they are the last resting place of two brothers who fought a duel and killed each other for the wife of one of them who was unfaithful to her husband. Nor does tradition stop there, but mingling fancy with fact, declares that on the anniversary day, or rather night, of this unholy duel, both brothers come out of their graves to wage again their desperate combat from midnight until dawn.

At this same spot I witnessed a combat of which I am about to relate the details. It is now a full year since this fight took place, and yet I have not hitherto mentioned a single word of it in my diary.

No matter. Have I not said that I did not write with the idea of printing? It is a provision of youth which I make for my old age. On reading over these letters in ten, twenty, thirty years, if in ten, twenty, or thirty years I am still alive, perhaps I may succeed in recalling to my mind the sensations of the past, in rekindling memories long since dead, and in returning again along the flowery paths and the cool groves of my springtime. God grant it! Such a glorious gift is youth! Unhappily we only realize its value when we have lost it forever.

Well, more than a year ago, on 4 May in the year 18—, several officers of our regiment met together to celebrate the birthday of the Aide-de-camp. Just as we were going to sit down to table, the Colonel sent for our host.

'Gentlemen,' said the latter, 'it is not likely to be for anything very important or anything that will detain me long, as I took the orders from the Colonel this very morning. Sit down and begin, as breakfast is ready; my cook would die of vexation if you let his dishes get cold.'

The company promised to sit down to table in ten minutes, if in ten minutes the Aide-de-camp had not returned. The cook, on being consulted, replied that he would answer for the breakfast if his master did not overstep the limit of ten minutes, and the Aide-de-camp went away, promising on his word of honour to come back as soon as possible.

While waiting for their host, and to pass the ten minutes which always seem so long while awaiting a meal, the officers began relating their most scandalous garrison stories. The manservant Koloff cleared the adjoining room and prepared the tables and the cards, conjecturing that gambling for madly extravagant stakes would be the only amusement which would not seem insipid after a breakfast at which each man had made up his mind to vie with his neighbour as to who would eat best and drink most. The feats of valour performed in this respect by unfortunate officers whose sole recreation in certain cantonments are wine and good living, are well known.

At the tenth minute everyone was about to sit down to table, when, on the declaration of the cook that breakfast could be kept waiting five minutes longer without too great inconvenience, a further short period of delay was granted to the absentee.

At the fourteenth minute the long-expected host appeared on the threshold, and was greeted by a unanimous shout of 'Hurrah for Andrev Mikaelovitch!'

'Hurrah! yes gentlemen, hurrah!' replied he, 'but it is at table with glass in hand that we must cry hurrah! Sit down! Sit down!'

Each guest had had his place appointed beforehand; in a moment, therefore, the important manoeuvre was carried out.

'And now,' asked Sub-Lieutenant Stamm, 'can you tell us, without indiscretion, Andrev Mikaelovitch, what the Colonel had to tell you that was so pressing?'

'To be sure, and I shall repeat it to you all the more willingly, because, if I did not tell you the news, you would know it on leaving here, or even before then. A new officer is being transferred from the Guards into our regiment, and is to fill the vacant captaincy.'

'His name?' came from two or three voices.

'Lieutenant Zodomirsky.'

'And when does he arrive?' asked Major Belayeff.

'He has arrived; I saw him at the Colonel's, who sent for me to introduce him to me.'

'What is he like?' asked young Cornet Naletoff.

'Oh! he looks all right. He seems to love his profession; he arrived simultaneously with the Imperial ordinance appointing him to the post. So you see he has lost no time. He is very anxious to become acquainted with you all, so I have invited him to dine with us, as I presume we shall make a day of it. But can you understand this? Although he had just alighted from his chaise, he was in full dress; he had travelled in parade uniform. Deuce take it! they seem to be pretty strict where he comes from!'

'Gentlemen,' I ventured to say, 'Zodomirsky will have thought that, calling for the first time on the Colonel on coming to join his regiment, he could not present himself at his house as we others do, in simple undress.'

'Faugh!' cried Major Belayeff. 'I detest these dandy officers and ceremonious military men; full dress is all very well when one is on guard at the Emperor's Palace. But you have not told us the impression he made upon you, Andrev Mikaelovitch.'

'Why yes! I think I have given you a hint already,' the Aide-de-camp said lightly. 'He is a very good-looking fellow, with all the manners of the Guards, you know. He spoke the purest French, and fired off a whole string of polite nothings. Oh! he is a regular drawing-room man, anybody can see, a very fine gentleman, like everything that comes to us from St Petersburg. But, on the whole, I think he is a very decent fellow, and one who will soon get used to our ways.'

'Our fair friend, Marianna Ravensky, was well posted. She told me a week ago that this fop was being sent out to us. But, by the way, you ought to know him, Captain,' continued Mikaelovitch, turning to me, 'you come from the Guards too, and you were in the same regiment with him.'

'Quite true,' I answered, 'we were at the Military School together; he shaped well then, and was above all a very good-hearted chap; he was a favourite with all his comrades, and got on well all round. I do not know what he has become now; but at that time he was a fine young fellow, but of an irritable and hasty temper.'

'What the Captain says must be true; it agrees exactly with Madame Ravensky's estimate of the man; she assures me he is a keen duellist. "*Noli me tangere!*" Well, he will be in his element here,' went on Stamm. 'The duel is quite a family affair there, and the Tombs of the Two Brothers our Bois de Boulogne. Welcome, Monsieur Zodomirsky.' These words Stamm pronounced with visible, though restrained, anger.

'Well, you're the man who will have to set him to rights, Stamm,' said the Aide-de-camp. 'Zodomirsky is more in your way here than in anyone else's; if a ready-made Captain had not been sent down to us, Lieutenant Dmitry would have been promoted to the captaincy and you to the lieutenancy – God knows when your turn will come now.'

'I would willingly remain another year in the rank I fill, though I have occupied it a pretty long time, if I stayed there to do a good comrade a service; but I admit that it goes against the grain to see the pet lamb of some minister's mistress promoted over my head. Therefore, let Monsieur Zodomirsky look out for himself. Let him be irritable and hasty, if that's his temperament, but not towards me, or I will take it upon myself to quiet him.'

'Is he ruined, that he is leaving the Guards?' asked Cornet Naletoff.

'Ruined! Nothing of the kind!' replied Stamm. 'Why, Madame Ravensky told me he had just inherited something like twenty-thousand roubles a year from an old aunt. No, he is consumptive, poor devil! If he joins us at one of our good sittings of thirty-six hours and is able to hold his own without flinching, he may well lose what little breath he has left.

'Struth, I'm sorry for you, Captain Zodomirsky, but Veuve Clicquot will
not listen to the excuses of consumptives, and for medicine she knows
only one prescription – a bottle of champagne divided into five glasses to
be drunk every five minutes, and the same the hour following, always
doubling the dose, until the basket is empty. Damn it! we get drunk seven
times a week, and you can all bear me out, gentlemen, that Andrev
Mikaelovitch thinks that's not often enough. What a pity there is not an
eighth day in the week, eh, Andrev Mikaelovitch?'

'Pardieu! the less you say about that the better, Stamm! You are ten
years my junior, but I think that if the wine we have drunk were put
back into cask, you would be as much my elder in casks as I am yours in
years!'

'Come, gentlemen, let us adjourn to the card room, and take with us
our half-emptied bottles. Koloff will be cooking dinner while we are
playing,' and the company rose from table and passed into the card room.

'You take the bank, Major Belayeff,' said Naletoff, 'and put down
one-hundred roubles; that will be enough; we are not unreasonable
fellows. The hen only eats a grain at a time, you know.'

The Major sat down, drew one-hundred roubles from his pocket,
placed the coin, or rather the paper, in front of him; each officer made
his stake, and sat down, in turn, at the same table as the Major.

Sub-Lieutenant Stamm, who was far from being a rich man, had just
lost a stake of sixty roubles when Koloff announced Captain Zodomirsky.

CHAPTER II

THE NEW OFFICER

At this name, which aroused so many different emotions, everybody turned round, and the newcomer appeared in the doorway.

Stamm muttered a 'Let him go to the devil!' as he pushed the sixty roubles over to the Major, and dived deep into his pocket to find thirty or forty more.

'So you have come at last!' exclaimed the Aide-de-camp, Andrev Mikaelovitch, as he rose from his seat and went forward to meet Zodomirsky. 'You are welcome.'

Then, turning to us, 'Here are your new comrades, Captain Zodomirsky,' continued Andrev Mikaelovitch. 'They are good fellows, one and all, and gallant Hussars, who will never disgrace their country, I dare swear.'

'Gentlemen,' said Zodomirsky, 'I am happy and proud to have at last managed to join your regiment; for years it has been the goal of my ambitions. If I am welcome, as you are polite enough to tell me I am, I shall be the happiest man in the world.'

Then perceiving me, his old acquaintance, in the midst of all his new comrades, 'Ah! good day, Captain!' he continued, holding out his hand. 'Fate brings us together again. You have not forgotten an old friend, I hope.'

As he said these words to me with a smile, Stamm, to whom his back was turned, darted a look full of ferocious hatred at him.

Without a word, I extended my hand to Zodomirsky. It was painful to me to think that a man who had done no harm to any of us, and whose only crime was what he had just owned to, namely, that he had desired to serve in our regiment, was for that reason, from the very first day of his joining, threatened with death. I was quite prepared to stand up for Zodomirsky, and I returned Stamm, as I might have done to a mortal enemy, the look he had just flung at the other. Stamm was absorbed in his game; he had just risked a second stake and had lost another twenty roubles, half of the whole sum he had before him.

No one in the regiment liked Stamm – he was cold and taciturn; he had never been intimate, perhaps from his fault, perhaps from ours, with any of us. As for myself, his words full of bitterness against Zodomirsky, whom he did not know, and which showed his annoyance at seeing him fill the vacancy in the regiment, had disgusted me more than I can say. Indeed they had created a bad impression not only upon me, but on all of us.

Zodomirsky was offered a cigar; he accepted it pleasantly, lit it at the cigar of the officer who happened to be nearest to him, and began to chat with his new comrades. The conversation turned to the life officers of the Guards led at St Petersburg contrasted with that of officers stationed in the provinces, on Poland, on women, horses, dogs and sport.

'Will you soon leave us to join the squadron?' asked Major Belayeff, who knew that Zodomirsky was rich, and wanted to draw his attention to the cards.

'No, Major,' replied Zodomirsky, bowing to the man who addressed him, 'no; I wish to remain as long as possible with you, gentlemen.'

And as he said this, he turned towards us and bowed to us all collectively with a charming smile. Then he went on, 'I wanted to see something of your service at close quarters, and learn my duties. Your instructor, Monsieur Ravensky, with whom I spent the winter at St Petersburg, has been most kind to me. Even before my arrival – and it is only about a week that he has known of my nomination – he has had quarters prepared for me near his own home, on the summit of your hill. I have a good fireplace, which is a necessity to me, even during the summer, on account of my bad health; my horses will soon be brought over; I shall ride, it is a passion with me; I have an excellent cook, a passable library, a small garden; I shall put up a shooting gallery, and live quiet as a hermit and happy as a king; it is a life that suits me, the life I dreamt of down yonder, even in the midst of the pleasure of St Petersburg.'

'Ah, ah! so you do a lot of pistol shooting?' said Stamm with an accent so strange, accompanied with so sardonic a smile that Zodomirsky, who had turned towards him, looked at him with astonishment.

'Why yes! it is my habit every morning to fire a dozen shots,' replied Zodomirsky.

Then, after a second's silence, he turned away from Stamm.

'Has this occupation such attractions for you, then?' asked Stamm in a voice in which there remained not a trace of emotion. 'I understand a man practising with his gun in order to make himself a good shot when pursuing game; but I cannot see the use of practising pistol shooting.'

Zodomirsky perceived instantly that Stamm had deliberately made up his mind to force a quarrel upon him. His features lit up; his cheeks, usually pale, became suffused with a sudden flush. He turned for the second time towards Stamm and answered quietly, but in a firm voice, 'I think, monsieur, that you are wrong in saying that it is a waste of time to learn how to use a pistol. In our garrison life, often an imprudent word leads to an encounter between comrades; in that case, he who is known to be a good shot exercises a certain wholesome restraint on indiscreet persons who amuse themselves by asking silly questions.'

'Oh! that is not always a sufficient reason, Captain! In a duel, as in everything else in the world, one must take one's chance. In any case, I maintain my first opinion, and consider that an honest man should not take so many precautions.'

'And why so?' asked Zodomirsky, whose face had returned to its normal pallor.

'I will explain that to you in a moment,' replied Stamm. 'Do you play cards, Captain?'

'Why do you ask?'

'Oh! it is a silly question, no doubt! Well, I am going to try and make my parable plain enough for everyone to understand it. No one is ignorant of the fact that there are players who have the happy knack, but bad habit, of helping luck by a clever shuffle of the cards or an adroit cut. Well, in my opinion, to be certain of a bull's eye at every shot is exactly the same thing, the only difference is this – that, in the first case, a man robs his neighbour of his money, and in the second, of his life.'

Then he added, but in such a way as to detract nothing from the insolence of what he had said, 'I don't say this for you in particular, Captain; I am speaking generally.'

'You have already said too much as it is, monsieur,' exclaimed Zodomirsky. 'In consequence, I shall beg Captain Alexis Stephanovitch to settle this affair with you.'

Then, turning to me and holding out his hand, 'You will not refuse me this favour, will you?' he said to me.

'Agreed, Captain,' Stamm quickly answered, 'but do not be too sure you will win; you practise every day, you yourself have said so, while I, I never touch a pistol except when I fight; we will try to make the chances equal; I shall come to an understanding with Alexis Stephanovitch.'

Then, as he had lost even his last rouble, he got up; and addressing himself to our host, 'Goodbye, Andrev Mikaelovitch; to give you more room at the table, I am going to dine with the Colonel.'

And so saying, Stamm left the room without anyone attempting to detain him.

The deepest silence had been maintained throughout this altercation; to take part in it, for or against, would have meant being involved in the quarrel. Only, when Stamm had gone, old Captain Pravdine said, addressing himself to everyone, 'Gentlemen, we cannot possibly let them fight.'

Zodomirsky gently put his hand on his arm. 'Allow me to observe, Captain,' said he, 'that among you all, I am what is called a newcomer; I am not yet known in the regiment, I have not yet proved myself. It is therefore impossible for me to allow this quarrel to pass without fighting; the insult is great, I realize it to the full. I really do not know what I have done to this gentleman, but one thing is very clear, that he wants an affair with me; do not let us deprive him of the satisfaction, and, since this is the first occasion which presents itself for me to be agreeable to him, well, allow me to avail myself of it.'

'Stamm is in love with Madame Ravensky,' said Cornet Naletoff, who, in contrast to Stamm, was winning at cards; 'the lady does not respond, occupied as she is in dreaming of Zodomirsky; and Stamm is jealous; that is the reason, if not the excuse, for his outbreak. It is impossible for a man to seek a quarrel with another for the simple reason that he takes rank before him. In any case, God keep you, Captain,' he added, addressing himself to Zodomirsky. 'I detest Germans in general and him in particular.'

'I admit that Madame Ravensky thinks kindly of me,' Zodomirsky replied simply, 'I have never had any but friendly relations with her husband; besides, I have known her personally for a long time, and in every circumstance I have striven to prove that I am her friend. In addition to which I am glad of this event, whatever the consequences may be, since it is to him that I owe a proof of your sympathy, gentlemen; I thank you therefore with all my heart, and you in particular, my dear Captain,' he added, holding out his hand to Pravdine.

'Take your seats, gentlemen! take your seats!' cried Andrev Mikaelovitch. 'A glass of cognac or of kummel first of all. Come here, Monsieur Zodomirsky, here, beside me, I beg; you are our guest today; let us hope, then, that God will permit us to spend this day together and many others after this.'

Then turning to the other officers, 'Seat yourselves where you will, gentlemen; you know that you are at home. The soup, Koloff, the soup, and be quick about it!'

Koloff brought in a large soup tureen full of 'tchi', which everyone attacked with gusto.

The dinner was a lively one; everybody appeared to have forgotten Stamm, although evidently everybody was thinking of the insult which he had given; Zodomirsky alone was visibly a little sad.

After having drunk to the health of the host, a toast was proposed in honour of the guest. Zodomirsky seemed deeply touched at this attention, doubly significant at this moment; he thanked the officers in a voice full of emotion, and his face lit up with gratitude.

Instead of coffee, grog and punch were brought in; Captain Pravdine drank one glass only of cold grog, then addressed the officers. 'Gentlemen,' he said, 'who is coming with me? I am going to the Ravenskys'.'

'I will accompany you, Captain,' said Zodomirsky; 'it is absolutely necessary that I should see Monsieur Ravensky this evening. Alexis Stephanovitch,' he added, turning to me, 'since Monsieur Stamm – you call him Stamm, I think?'

I nodded.

'Since Monsieur Stamm knows that you are my second, and appears to have accepted your intervention, call upon Monsieur Stamm, make all arrangements with him, accept all his conditions, his conditions will be mine; then return to my house; we will come back there with the Captain for tea; the first to arrive will wait for the others. The Captain will sleep at my house; in all probability we shall have to be up early. It is agreed, is it not?'

'All right,' said Pravdine, nodding his head affirmatively.

'Gentlemen,' said several voices, 'tomorrow we shall find ourselves at the Tomb of the Two Brothers; you will send us word at what hour the meeting takes place, will you not?'

'Many thanks, gentlemen,' replied Zodomirsky. 'Alexis Stephanovitch will comply with your wishes on his return from Monsieur Stamm; come, and you will bid an eternal farewell to one of us.'

The officers in a body accompanied Zodomirsky as far as the door of the Ravenskys'; on separating, each shook hands with him as with a relative or a friend. I went to Stamm's house.

He was expecting me; his conditions were such as I had foreseen.

Two swords were to be planted a pace apart. Each man was to extend his arm full length and fire at the word 'three'; only one pistol would be loaded.

I tried to argue and to obtain a different mode of combat, but Stamm would not budge from his resolution.

'I do not wish to offer a victim to Monsieur Zodomirsky, but an adversary,' said he. 'We shall fight according to my conditions, or not at all; only, if we do not fight, it will be proved that Monsieur Zodomirsky is brave only when sure of his shot.'

With this dilemma put before me, hesitation was no longer a possibility; besides, Zodomirsky had ordered me to accept all Stamm's conditions.

I returned to Zodomirsky's house; he was not yet in. As a distraction from the sombre thoughts which filled my mind, I examined the young Captain's room.

It was furnished almost luxuriously; the floor was entirely covered by a magnificent carpet; there were flowers at every window and on every table. The whole effect was rich but simple, and arranged with taste. One felt that the hand of a woman had put each one of these things in its place. I drew an easy chair close to the balcony to look over the plain; on the left were to be seen, receding in the distance until almost lost to sight, the villages which I have mentioned; in the centre of each rose its ancient church gilded by the last rays of the setting sun. The sky was covered with heavy clouds. A storm was approaching; the peasants, aided by their wives, were hastening to put the hay into ricks before the rain; the storm rose rapidly, large drops began to fall, the thunder rolled.

In a moment the plain was deserted.

Just then Pravdine and Zodomirsky returned.

I sprang forward to meet him.

'Pardon me, Captain, if I have kept you waiting,' said Zodomirsky to me, 'but it is not my fault. The Ravenskys have detained us, the husband with his ideas about economy, the wife with her charming conversation. I have met few women so delightful as she is. But, gentlemen, don't you feel it is damp in here? Trophime, close the balcony windows, and bring in the tea.'

Then, suddenly turning to me, 'Well!' he asked, 'what did Stamm say?'

I acquainted him with the unreasonable demands of his adversary. He listened coldly. Only when I had finished did a sad smile cross his face. He wiped his forehead; his eyes shone like those of a man in fever.

'I had foreseen that,' he said, drawing up chairs for Pravdine and me, and placing himself between us. 'There was nothing else for him to do. You have accepted, I presume?'

'Didn't you instruct me to do so?'

'Positively,' replied Zodomirsky. 'Trophime, I have already asked you to bring in tea.'

Pravdine, instead of tea, poured a tot of rum into his glass, lit his pipe, and began to give an account of his stay in Paris in 1814.

I had heard this story a hundred times, consequently I paid little attention to it. Zodomirsky, on the contrary, wishing to prove to Pravdine that he was listening to him, from time to time asked him a question, but rather, one felt, from politeness than from curiosity.

Pravdine doubtless noticed this, because he broke off short, suppressing a good number of details that I knew, and replacing them with this sacramental phrase, 'Ah! we had gay times then; I did not worry about a thing, and lived like a lord.'

After Pravdine's story a gloomy silence succeeded.

I went to sit near the fireplace; Pravdine retired to an easy chair near a window.

Zodomirsky, by a movement of the body, rolled his chair along on its back legs, so bringing himself close to a table upon which he leant his elbows.

Sitting in this position he had the door immediately in front of him.

Suddenly, the door half opened, and we saw Trophime, who, with the evident intention of speaking to his master, remained however on the threshold; his left hand held the door; with his right he supported himself against the wall, as if forbidding someone's entrance into the room.

Zodomirsky, absorbed in his reverie, did not see him.

'Sir!' said Trophime, in a half whisper, 'Sir!'

'Well!' asked Zodomirsky.

'Will you be good enough to come, please.'

'You have something to tell me?'

'Yes, with your permission.'

'Speak out, you know that I detest being disturbed when I am comfortable. These gentlemen are my friends.'

'Sir, it is on secret and important business.'

Zodomirsky had half risen with his habitual indolence of movement, when Trophime, yielding to a power invisible to us, relinquished his post at the door, and admitted a woman covered with a black cloak and with a hood drawn over her head.

Water was streaming from her clothes.

She unclasped her cloak, took off her hood, and let them fall on the carpet.

Her comb, which had caught in her hood, rolled with it on to the floor.

Her face was pale, her hair hung down; a small brown holland wrapper was fastened round her figure.

We recognized Madame Ravensky.

CHAPTER III

MARIANNA

This apparition produced a different effect on each of the persons present.

I remained in my place, looking at her in amazement; Pravdine rose, passed softly behind her, picked up her cloak and gave her her comb; Zodomirsky sprang towards her and seized her two hands.

'What have you done, good God! and why are you here?' he said to her.

'Why am I here, Georges?' she exclaimed. 'You ask me that, when this night is perhaps the last of your life. Why am I here? To bid you farewell, unhappy man! I saw you only two hours ago, and you told me nothing of what is to take place tomorrow morning. Was it kind of you, my dearest?'

'But I am not alone here,' replied Zodomirsky in a low voice, 'think of it, Marianna. Your reputation, your good name——'

'Oh! are you not everything in the world to me, Georges? My only care, I may almost say my only duty, is to love you.'

She placed her two hands on Zodomirsky's shoulders, and leant her head against his breast.

We turned to leave the room, Pravdine and I.

'Ah! stay, gentlemen,' said she, raising her head; 'you have seen me here; I have nothing to conceal from you. Besides, you are his friends, and his friends are not strangers to me. Remain, therefore, and by remaining, you will, I am sure, be able to help me. I have important business to discuss with him.'

Zodomirsky pressed her to his heart, but she gently pushed him away and sat down in the chair where her lover was sitting at the moment she came in.

She threw back her head, coiled up her hair and fastened it with her comb.

I have never in my life seen anything more beautiful than this woman throwing herself back with a violent movement, her eyes wet with tears, her mouth half open, her voice choked with sobs, her neck swollen with the strain. The tempest of the heart had disturbed the harmony of her

features, but without disfiguring them. She had bent under the
unexpected blow like a flower in a storm: but this blow, terrible though it
was, had not broken her heart. One could read in her expression a
remnant of hope. There was power and determination in her dark eyes.
She had come, not to bid adieu to Zodomirsky, but to make a last effort
to save him.

Zodomirsky walked with slow steps up and down the room.

He stopped several times in front of Madame Ravensky as if about to
question her; but, each time he turned away without a word; it was easy
to see that something embarrassed him.

She looked at him fixedly, and, with feminine intuition, answered his
thought.

'Do not be afraid of anything,' she said in a low tone as if ashamed of
her words, and without looking at Zodomirsky. 'He has gone to
Kremenetz; everyone was asleep when I left.'

'Alone? How imprudent!'

'No, with Dina.'

The woman who went so bravely to her ruin, who risked more than
her life, her reputation, became timid as a child when she had to speak
the name of the man whom she had betrayed; therefore his name had not
passed her lips. She had not hesitated to acknowledge her love before me
and Pravdine, but when, in order to answer Zodomirsky's thought, she
should have pronounced the name of her husband, she shrank from doing
so. In the same way the most shameless brigand, when relating to the
judges the details of his crime, never pronounces the name of his victim.
With him, the man whom he has killed is always 'he'.

When Marianna began to speak, Zodomirsky stopped (I have said that
he was pacing up and down the room) and listened. Then, when she had
finished, he resumed his walking, took one more turn and came back to
her, addressing her in a tone of tender reproach.

'What a fatal idea is this, my poor Marianna!' he said. 'Why, your
presence might take from me the firmness I need.'

'Oh! you will not die, Georges,' she cried, 'you will not destroy two
lives by a senseless death! Have you not given me your word to sacrifice it
to my happiness! No, Georges, you will not die, because you will not
fight with Stamm – I implore you, I beg you, I demand it. Your life
belongs to me. I have bought it by my love, by my sacrifices; it is no
longer yours; you are mine, Georges, do you hear? You belong to me for
ever, you yourself have said so.'

'Marianna! in Heaven's name do not torture me like this! Can I refuse
to answer an insult? I should be dishonoured, lost! Were I guilty of such
cowardice, the shame of it would kill me, more surely, believe me, than
Stamm's bullet.'

'Georges,' rejoined Madame Ravensky, 'have I ever spoken to you of my sacred duties when you asked for my love? Have I said a word of my dishonour, of my reputation, risked, stained, lost? No! I have surrendered myself without reserve, without conditions, without complaints, without this cold egoism with which you now calculate the extent of the sacrifice I am exacting from you. Oh! Georges! Georges! compare what I have done with what you refuse to do, and compare your love and mine!'

Then seeing that Georges remained silent, and turned his head away, 'Captain,' said she, addressing herself to Pravdine, 'you are looked upon in the regiment as a man of honour; you should be a good judge in affairs of honour; listen to me; I appeal to you and submit in advance to the judgment you pronounce. Take pity on me, Captain, and tell him that such a duel can be refused, make him understand that it is not a fair engagement, that it is the duel of an assassin; speak, speak, Captain! And if he does not listen to me, perhaps he will listen to you.'

Pravdine was touched, his cheeks trembled, his lips twitched under his grey moustache, his eyes grew wet with tears.

He rose, approached Madame Ravensky, raised her hand respectfully, and in a trembling voice, 'I would willingly die to spare you pain, Madame,' said he, 'but to advise Monsieur Zodomirsky to be unworthy of his uniform by refusing this duel is an impossible thing. Each of the adversaries, your friend as well as Stamm, has the right to propose his conditions. But, whatever the conditions may be, the Captain is placed in circumstances which render the duel indispensable; but, you must remember that he is a clever pistol shot; to refuse Stamm's conditions would be to show too plainly that he counts on his skill.'

While Pravdine was speaking, Madame Ravensky looked at him attentively, trying to read the depth of his thought, hoping to find there some sympathy for her entreaty; but, from the moment she understood that she must not reckon upon him as an auxiliary, she ceased to listen, so that the Captain's last words fell upon her ears without penetrating to her mind.

She had fallen pensive, and the light faded little by little from her eyes.

As to Zodomirsky's face, it expressed a quiet submission to fate, which he had not the strength, or rather not the will, to resist.

A gloomy silence fell on the room; one would have said that the four persons in it were dumb. But this silence was the hush that precedes a storm. Madame Ravensky had sunk back in a chair; she got up swiftly, white as death, and, although her face was apparently calm, one could see, by its lividness, the agony which she was enduring. She came and stood in front of Zodomirsky.

'Listen, Georges,' she said in a firm voice, 'my mind is made up. Do you remember that night at St Petersburg when you implored me to go away with you to Finland, to find some retreat there which would hide us from the eyes of the world, and there, unknown, forgotten, alone, to live for one another, far from the world, without ever casting our eyes back to it? I did not refuse you, seeing that I have never been able to refuse you anything, but you yourself understood that it was very difficult for me to break all the ties of blood and friendship which bound me to Russia, and you had pity on me; for in reality no one separated us, no one prevented us from loving each other; now, it is another thing – well, yes, I understand that you are bound to fight; I even admit that you cannot refuse the conditions of your adversary; but, in admitting the duel under those conditions, it separates us inevitably; either you will be killed, and that perhaps is the surest means of our being reunited; or you will kill him, and then, that means degradation, exile, Siberia. Well, today, it is I who tell you, Georges; I am ready to follow you anywhere – do not look at me so sternly; no, Georges, listen to all I have to say. You sacrifice everything to the conventionalities of society. Let us leave it, then, and to recompense you for that loss of respect due to barbarous customs, you will find in me an inexhaustible mine of love, deep, true, devoted. I will surround you with such thoughtfulness, such tenderness, such care as can only come from the woman who not only adores you, but who combines gratitude with adoration. If I have committed a fault before God and before men, that fault I will redeem by unbounded devotion, superhuman love. You know very well that he does not love me, that he never has loved me, that he married me not for my youth, or my beauty, but my fortune; you know very well that he had such influence over my father, that my poor father, in uniting us, imagined that he was securing my happiness. Well, according to the laws of our Church, we may separate; I shall buy my liberty by giving up to him half – three-quarters – of my fortune; then I will become your wife, and we will be happy, Georges.'

'Stop, Marianna, in God's name, stop!' cried Georges. 'I cannot endure this torture; you do not know what you are asking me! I am an officer; if I go away with you, I do not run away, I desert; wherever I am, I shall be found. Do you understand that word – "deserter"? It is ignominy, ignominy doubled by the cause of the desertion. I shall have deserted so as not to fight a duel! Oh! would you make me fall so low that you yourself should come to be ashamed of me? Ashamed of me, think of that! It means to be no longer able to love me; because, tell me, I ask you to your face, you, a woman of honour, as I am a man of honour, would you be able to love a dishonoured man?'

Madame Ravensky grew pale; a new thought lit up her face, and stamped itself upon her features, illuminated with unnatural brilliance.

She rose and took her cloak which lay on the back of Pravdine's chair. 'You are right, Georges,' said she, drawing her hood over her face. 'It is not I who would no longer love you, it is you who would hate me.'

Zodomirsky made a gesture which indicated that he was too sure of himself ever to arrive at that extremity.

She saw this gesture and understood it.

'Oh! if you did not hate me, I should hate myself,' said she, 'for having placed you in so cruel a position. We must resign ourselves to our fate; give me your hand, Georges. We shall see each other again. No, you will not die; God will not be so cruel, or so unjust; otherwise I should doubt His existence. Till tomorrow, till tomorrow, my love!'

She fell on his neck, clung to him with the deepest sadness, but without tears, without sobs; one could see that her thoughts wandered vague and distraught, like wisps of cloud driven hither and thither by a tempest.

She wished to go back alone, but Zodomirsky drew her arm through his and took her to her home.

The storm had passed, the rain had ceased, the plain stretched clear in the moonlight.

When Zodomirsky returned, we opened the windows, and sat out on the balcony to refresh ourselves a little.

'Go and lie down, gentlemen,' said Zodomirsky on hearing the church clock chime. 'There is one divan in this room, another in my bedroom. Trophime will give you all you want. I must write several letters before going to bed, and make some sort of a will in case anything should happen to me. We shall be awakened tomorrow at four o'clock, and at five we shall be at the appointed place.'

I felt so fatigued that I did not wait to be told twice; I went into Zodomirsky's room, Pravdine retired to the drawing-room, and the master of the house withdrew into his dressing-room.

The chill of the morning woke me. I looked at the window; day was beginning to dawn. I jumped off the divan, intending to go into Zodomirsky's room, but stopped short. It is cruel to wake a man to tell him 'It is time to die!' With some hesitation I entered his dressing-room, the door of which stood ajar; two candles were still burning, and mingled their waning light with the pale glimmer of the breaking day.

I cast my eyes on Zodomirsky's bed – it was not disturbed, he had not gone to bed. The carpet which covered the floor deadened the sound of my footsteps; I was therefore able to come near to Zodomirsky, almost to touch him, without being heard.

He was leaning on his elbows close to the open window.

'You have not slept,' I said. 'That is not right; on the night preceding a duel a little rest is necessary.'

'Ah! you are already up,' said Zodomirsky, without answering what I was saying to him. 'Is it time?'

He was pale, but his face expressed less physical than mental fatigue.

Would he be in a state to endure the last crisis? I asked myself with a certain anxiety on seeing how tired he was even before reaching the ground.

Evidently he read my anxiety in my face, because he smiled and pressed my hand with a strength of which I should have thought him incapable. 'It seems you do not know me,' said he. 'Don't be afraid, you will not have to blush for your protégé.'

We could hear Pravdine getting up. I went into the drawing-room; Trophime brought in the tea. Zodomirsky had remained in his dressing-room; I opened the door to let him know that tea was ready.

He was on his knees, praying.

I was afraid that he might be annoyed at being surprised; but he was not in the least; he gave a nod which implied, 'I shall be with you in a moment.'

A few minutes later he came out of the dressing-room, his face quite serene. 'Are the horses ready?' he asked, in a voice in which it was impossible to distinguish the least emotion.

I looked out of the window; a chaise with four horses was drawn up a few steps away from the entrance; I beckoned to the man in charge, and he drove up to the door.

'Oh! we have time enough,' said Pravdine. 'You can see the whole plain from here, and there is no one either on the road or at the rendezvous.'

'Good!' said Zodomirsky, 'we may as well go at once; gentlemen, if you are ready, so am I.'

'Come, let us go,' said I, 'the Captain is right; better arrive too soon than that they should have to wait for us.'

We got into the carriage; Zodomirsky insisted on our sitting at the back, while he sat in front.

'Drive on!' he said to the coachman.

'Where to, your Excellency?'

'Ah true! I forgot; to the Tomb of the Two Brothers.'

The carriage drove off.

CHAPTER IV

THE DUEL

Zodomirsky was not sad, only from time to time he grew pensive, and seemed to meditate over the thoughts which filled his mind. I followed each of his movements for, taking a keen interest in the young man as I did, none of his sufferings escaped me.

The last day of a condemned man is awful, no doubt; but his sufferings are passive and without struggle; he must submit to a fate from which he cannot escape; while on the contrary, Zodomirsky, insulted, having the choice of weapons, could say one word, only one, and by changing the conditions of the combat, change also the chances of it. What an effort of will was called for to refrain from uttering that word! And yet that is what this brave young man was doing. As for myself, I admit that some insane ideas passed through my brain; I felt inclined to advise him to leave the service, sell his property and go away with his mistress. But I scrupled to overthrow this resolution which aroused in me such genuine respect.

I was disturbed from my reflections by Pravdine.

'Ah!' he said, 'here comes Andrev Mikaelovitch's troika – yes, upon my word! it is he with another of ours; and there is young Naletoff galloping up on his Circassian horse. Good! the others are behind; come – we did well to start when we did.'

The carriage came down the hill by a winding road, the descent being too steep for anyone to attempt a straight course; in its turnings it passed in front of the Ravenskys' house. When opposite this house I could not resist looking up; the poor woman was at her window, motionless as a statue; she did not even bow to us.

'Faster! faster!' Zodomirsky called out to the coachman.

This was the only sign by which I knew that he, too, had seen Marianna.

The order given by Zodomirsky made the horses fly; soon we had outstripped the other carriages, and arrived at a little wood which was the usual meeting place for seconds and adversaries before proceeding to the place of combat.

Andrev Mikaelovitch rode up immediately after us. Within five minutes of our arriving we formed a group of about twenty persons.

Stamm had not yet arrived.

'Wait for Stamm,' said Major Belayeff to the aide-de-camp on his suggesting that we should repair at once to the Tomb of the Two Brothers, 'he is not late.'

He looked at his watch.

'See,' said he, 'the rendezvous is for five o'clock, and it is only five minutes to five.'

'There they are!' said Andrev Mikaelovitch, pointing in the direction of the second road which led from the base of the hill to the place where we were. In fact, a horseman was coming at full gallop, preceding an open carriage driven at full speed.

The rider was Stamm; in the carriage were his two seconds.

'Gentlemen,' said Zodomirsky, 'I think we may as well proceed to the Tomb of the Two Brothers. As everything is arranged beforehand it is useless to wait at a place where as a rule the conditions are discussed.'

As the rest of the way could only be done on foot, everyone dismounted, and waited on the duelling ground itself.

Zodomirsky leant against one of the two tombs. I carried the box containing his pistols.

The plain on which the two pyramids rise is fairly large; it was still somewhat veiled by the shades of night; but the first sunrays darting through the trees were beginning to shine upon it.

Soon we heard the sound of footsteps on the gravel; it was those of the newcomers.

They came on to the ground, Stamm walking first, a case of pistols in his hand.

He saluted Zodomirsky and the officers, put down his case, and asked, 'Who will give the word to fire, gentlemen?'

The two adversaries and the seconds turned towards the officers, who looked at each other in perplexity.

No one offered himself, no one wanted to pronounce that terrible word 'three' which meant death to a comrade.

'Major,' said Zodomirsky to Belayeff, 'do us this service, please.'

Thus appealed to, the Major did not like to refuse; he gave a sign of consent.

'Be good enough to point out the places, gentlemen,' went on Zodomirsky, giving me his sword and taking off his overcoat.

Then, when the places were marked out, 'Load, please.'

'As regards this last delay, it is unnecessary,' said Stamm. 'I have brought my pistols; one of the two is loaded, the other is only primed.'

'But these pistols, you are familiar with them,' said Pravdine.

'What does that matter?' replied Stamm. 'Monsieur Zodomirsky will choose which he pleases.'

'Very well,' said Zodomirsky, with a bow, 'let it be so.'

Belayeff drew his sword and dug it into the ground, between the Tombs of the Two Brothers; then he took the sword of another officer and planted it opposite to the other.

One single pace separated the two swords. Each adversary stood behind the sword, stretching out his arm above the hilt.

In this way each had his adversary's pistol six inches away from his heart.

While Belayeff was making these preparations, Stamm, in turn, unbuckled his sword and removed his overcoat. Stamm's seconds opened his case of pistols; Zodomirsky approached and without hesitation took the one nearest to him.

Then he proceeded to place himself behind one of the swords.

Stamm watched him with observant eyes; not a muscle of Zodomirsky's face moved, nothing in him indicated an appearance of emotion.

And yet there was not the least trace of posing in his attitude. It was the calmness of courage, the power of will.

'There is no doubt about it, he is a brave man!' muttered Stamm.

And taking up the pistol which Zodomirsky had left in the case he proceeded to place himself behind the other sword, opposite to his adversary.

They were both pale, but both unmoved. Perhaps anyone looking closely might have noticed a certain anxiety in Stamm's expression; but as the terrible moment approached Zodomirsky's face lit up and shone with an implacable resolve.

Pravdine was very excited; his cheeks were purple, he suffered visibly. My face, too, must have had a strange expression; I felt my heart beating to suffocation.

'Come, come, Major!' cried Pravdine to Belayeff.

Belayeff advanced.

All eyes were fixed upon him; we counted his steps as one counts the seconds between life and death.

He stepped close to the combatants. 'Are you ready, gentlemen?' asked he.

'We are waiting for you, Major,' Zodomirsky and Stamm said together. And each levelled his pistol at the other's breast, aiming at his heart.

A deathly silence hung over us.

Only the birds sang in the cluster of trees which stood forty feet away from the field of battle.

In the midst of this silence the Major's voice resounded, and made everyone shudder.

'One,' he said.

Then, at regular intervals, 'Two – three!'

The click of the hammer of Zodomirsky's pistol falling on the nipple was heard.

Then the priming was seen to take fire, but no report followed the flame.

The wind carried away the smoke.

Stamm had not fired, and still held the barrel of his pistol pointed at his adversary's breast.

'Fire!' said Zodomirsky, in a perfectly calm tone.

Pravdine, who held his naked sword in his right hand, flung it into his left with a convulsive movement.

'It is not for you to command, Monsieur Zodomirsky,' said Stamm; 'it is for me, on the contrary, to decide whether I shall fire or not. Besides, I do not yet know what I shall do; that will depend on the answer you give me.'

'Go on, then; but, in Heaven's name, say what you have to say, and get it over.'

'Never fear; I shall not take advantage of your patience.'

We were all attention.

'I did not come here to kill you, Monsieur,' continued Stamm. 'I came here with the recklessness of a man who does not hold to life, seeing that life has not fulfilled any of the promises that it made him. It is not the same with you, monsieur; you are rich, you are loved, you have a fine future before you, life must be dear to you. And yet, fate has decided against you; it is you who have to die, and not I. Well, Monsieur Zodomirsky, give me your word that, in future, you will not be so over-hasty in challenging your comrades, and I will not fire.'

'I was not over-hasty in challenging you,' replied Zodomirsky in the same quiet voice. 'The facts were otherwise; you wounded me by an outrageous comparison, and I had no choice but to challenge you; so fire, I do not want to bandy words with you.'

'No, Captain, you are mistaken, I have not insulted you. I said, do you not remember, "I do not speak for you in particular, I speak generally", I said that aloud, in front of all my comrades, and that should have been sufficient, it seems to me, for you not to take my words personally.'

'I suppose you are right, but to accept your conditions at the point of your pistol would be unworthy of a man of honour. Let us therefore bring the matter to a close, we have not come here to argue. Fire; when death is certain, delays are cruel; I am ready, fire.'

'My conditions cannot wound your honour,' insisted Stamm. 'I ask you to judge, Major,' added he, turning towards Belayeff, 'and submit myself, in advance, to your opinion; perhaps Monsieur will follow my example.'

'Monsieur Zodomirsky has remained firm and impassive in front of your pistol,' replied Major Belayeff. 'If he is not killed, it is not his fault; therefore, in my opinion he has acted as gallantly as it was possible for him to act; but my opinion is not decisive.'

Then, turning to the other officers present at the scene, 'Gentlemen,' asked Major Belayeff, 'can Monsieur Zodomirsky accept the prescribed conditions?'

'He can! he can!' cried the officers, 'without it injuring his honour in the least.'

Zodomirsky remained motionless, but his brow contracted.

'The Captain consents,' said old Pravdine coming forward.

'Yes, in future, he will be less hasty.'

'It is you who speak, Captain, and not Monsieur Zodomirsky,' said Stamm.

'Will you confirm my words, Monsieur Zodomirsky?' asked Pravdine almost imploringly.

'I consent,' said Zodomirsky in a scarcely intelligible voice.

'Hurrah! hurrah!' cried all the officers, delighted at the happy dénouement.

Two or three threw their caps up in the air.

'I am more delighted than anyone,' said Stamm, 'that everything should have ended as I wished. Now, Captain, we have finished; I have had an opportunity of showing you, that, in the face of a resolute man, the art of shooting counts as nothing in a duel, and that, if the chances are made equal, the good shot stands on the same footing as the bad one. There only remains for me now to prove to you that in any case I did not wish to kill you. I only wanted to see how you would look in the face of death. You have borne yourself bravely; accept my congratulations. The pistols were not loaded.'

And Stamm fired in his turn – only the priming exploded.

Zodomirsky uttered a cry that was more like a roar than anything else. 'By the soul of my father!' cried he, 'that is a fresh insult, and one far more offensive than the other. "Ah! it is ended", did you say? Not at all; it has only just begun. And this time, if I have to load the pistols myself, they will be loaded, do you hear!'

'No, Captain,' Stamm answered quietly. 'I have given you your life. I shall not take it away again. Take offence if you will, it does not matter much to me; I will not fight with you.'

'Then you will have to fight with me, Monsieur Stamm!' cried Pravdine, flinging his sword on the ground, and throwing off his overcoat, which he flung beside his sword, 'yes with me, and the conditions are of little consequence. Load the pistols gentlemen, quickly; one or both, as you will. As for you, Monsieur Stamm,' he continued, as he proceeded to take up his position in the place which Zodomirsky had occupied a few moments before, 'listen to me; you have acted like a miserable cur, do you hear? You have deceived Monsieur Zodomirsky and his seconds, and Providence will be unjust, if, in five minutes, your dead body does not lie there at my feet, beside this sword.'

Stamm was visibly taken aback; he had not imagined for a moment that the matter would finish in this manner. 'Very well,' said he, 'load the pistols.'

And he handed his to Major Belayeff.

'And if the Captain does not kill you, sir,' said Naletoff, walking up to where the swords lay, 'then I shall.'

'Or I! or I!' cried all the officers in one voice, approaching Stamm.

'I can't fight with you all,' replied Stamm. 'I have not insulted all of you, damn it! Choose one among you, and I will fight with him, otherwise it is not a duel, it is an assassination.'

'Set your mind at rest,' replied Major Belayeff, 'nothing will be done against you which the most scrupulous code of honour could complain of. All our officers are insulted; because, under their uniform, you have behaved like a cur. But you will not fight with them all; it is even probable that you will fight with no one. Stand aside, sir, you are on your trial. Monsieur Pravdine and Monsieur Stephanovitch come here,' he said.

We surrounded the Major, and judgment was found without discussion; everyone was of the same opinion.

Then the Major, who had acted as president, approached Stamm and said to him, 'Sir, in all that has just happened, you have acted contrary to all laws of honour, and the seconds would have every right to tear you to pieces. Were we legally your judges, we should condemn you, not perhaps to the most cruel, but to the most degrading of punishments. We are simply men wearing the same uniform as yourself, and we have but one right, to maintain the honour of the uniform we wear. You had weighed everything, calculated everything beforehand; your crime is therefore double, since it is premeditated. You have made Monsieur Zodomirsky go through all the mental torment of a man condemned to death, while you were perfectly at ease, you, knowing that the pistols were not loaded. Then last of all, when this man, who ought simply to have struck you in the face with his riding whip, when he gave you another opportunity of reinstating yourself by offering to fight with you, you refused the unexpected honour which he was doing you.'

'Load the pistols! load them!' exclaimed Stamm in exasperation; 'I shall fight with whoever you like.'

But the Major shook his head with a scornful smile. 'No, Lieutenant,' said he, 'you will never fight again with any of your comrades, nor will any of your comrades fight with you. You have stained your uniform, and must strip it off. None of us wish to serve with you any longer. The officers have requested me to tell you that, not wishing to inform against you to the government, they urge you to tender your resignation on the plea of ill health. The Surgeon-Major will sign all the necessary certificates. We are now at the 3rd of May; you have until the 3rd of June to leave the regiment.'

'Oh! certainly, I shall leave it, your regiment; not because it is your wish, but mine,' said Stamm, picking up his sword and throwing on his overcoat. Then, having buckled on his sword and donned his overcoat, Stamm sprang on to his horse's back and dashed off towards the town, hurling a last malediction on his comrades.

All the officers crowded round Zodomirsky.

He was sad, more than sad, gloomy, even more so than he had been when confronted by his enemy's pistol.

'Why did you make me consent to the conditions which this wretch exacted from me, gentlemen?' he said. 'But for you, I should never have accepted them.'

'Yes, you are right, it was our fault, Monsieur Zodomirsky,' replied the Major, 'and we, my comrades and myself, take the responsibility of it. You have acted nobly, and I tell you, in my name and in that of everyone here, Monsieur Zodomirsky, you are an honourable man.'

Then, turning to the officers, 'Let us be going, gentlemen,' added he. 'We shall take tea at Monsieur Zodomirsky's. Meanwhile, you, Andrev Mikaelovitch, go to the Colonel and inform him of all that has taken place.'

We took our places in the carriages; in the distance, Stamm could be seen riding up the hill at full gallop.

Zodomirsky threw a last look at him; his features contracted.

'I don't know,' he murmured.

'What?' Pravdine asked him.

'Why I have these presentiments; but I would rather his pistol had been loaded and he had fired.' He sighed heavily, pressed his two hands for a moment over his eyes, then shook his head and said to the coachman, 'Home!'

We returned by the same road as we had come, and again passed the home of the Ravenskys.

Each of us raised his eyes to the window; the window was still open, but Marianna was no longer there. Zodomirsky was ready to jump out of his carriage, but he did not do so; only, he murmured loud enough for me to hear, 'No, it would not be wise.'

After we had gone twenty paces he turned to me. 'Captain,' said he, 'you will not mind doing me a service, will you?'

'Whatever you wish, old fellow.'

'These gentlemen are going to my house. I cannot therefore keep them waiting; besides, Monsieur Ravensky may have returned; I rely upon you to go and tell Marianna the result of this foolish affair.'

'Whenever you wish.'

'The sooner the better.'

'At once.'

'Stop!' Zodomirsky cried to the coachman.

The man pulled up; I got out; Zodomirsky called out 'Thank you' to me, and continued on his way.

He returned to his house, and tea was served. He was lifting the first cup to his lips, when he saw me reappear at the door of the drawing-room.

I suppose I was pale, and no doubt my face betrayed my emotion because, careless whether he could be seen or heard, he rushed towards me exclaiming, 'Good God! Captain, what is the matter?'

I drew him out of the room.

'My dear friend,' I said to him, 'if you want to see your Marianna alive, make haste.'

'How so, in Heaven's name?'

'She was at her window; she saw Stamm pass; Stamm being alive, naturally you must be dead; she uttered one cry, and fell unconscious. Since then, she has not opened her eyes.'

'Oh!' cried Zodomirsky, 'my presentiments, my presentiments!'

He rushed out into the street bareheaded and without his sword.

Halfway down the staircase at Madame Ravensky's he met the doctor who had just left her room.

'Doctor!' he cried, stopping him, 'she is better, is she not?'

'Yes,' said the doctor; 'better; she is done with suffering.'

'Dead!' murmured Zodomirsky, turning ghastly white, and leaning against the wall to support himself, 'dead!'

'I was always telling her, poor soul, that, having an aneurism, she should avoid all emotion. Pshaw! these foolish women, they dream of nothing but emotions until at last they die of them. She has gone through some emotion this morning, I do not know what; she uttered a cry, fell backward, and all was over; but then, I ask you what was she doing at her window at six o'clock in the morning instead of being quiet and snug in bed. By the by,' the doctor went on, 'that reminds me, you had an unpleasant affair on hand this morning; it appears that it went off satisfactorily.'

But Zodomirsky was no longer listening to the doctor. He rushed upstairs, passed through the dining room and drawing-room, calling like a madman, 'Marianna! Marianna!'

At the door of her bedroom he found Dina, who tried to prevent his entrance.

He pushed her aside and went into the room.

Marianna was on her bed, silent, pale, still, her face calm as if in sleep, only a slight fringe of blood outlined her lips.

Zodomirsky fell on his knees beside her bed and seized her hand. It was cold; the end of a curl of black hair slipped through her stiffening fingers.

'My hair! my hair!' exclaimed Zodomirsky, bursting into sobs.

'Yes, your hair,' said the maid, 'your hair which she herself cut off when leaving you at St Petersburg. I always told her that that would bring ill-luck, either to one or the other.'

* * *

'Well,' I asked Monsieur Panovsky on returning him his manuscript the same evening, and before complimenting him on his narrative, so deeply had it interested me, 'is that how your story ends?'

'What more do you want?'

'I should like to know what became of Zodomirsky.'

'One person alone can give you positive information on the subject,' he said to me.

'Who is it?'

'On leaving Moscow you are going to the Monastery of Troitza?'

'Yes.'

'Ask for Brother Vasili, and if he is still living and consents to do, he can give you all the information you desire on this matter.'

So on leaving Moscow I went to the Monastery of Troitza, and my first question was to ask for Brother Vasili.

He had been dead three months; I was shown his grave.

That was all that the survivors could do for me.

I questioned them; no one knew his family name, nor the causes which had led him, at twenty-six years of age, to assume the robe of a monk.

They said vaguely that it was after some great sorrow caused by the death of a woman he loved.

THE ELUSIVE BIRD

There lingers at Marseilles an ancient and hallowed tradition, the origin of which is lost in the mists of time, a tradition to the effect that wild pigeons have been known to fly over the region. Now, all the Marseillese, who like the men of Aigues-Mortes, have retained of their many ancient municipal rights only that of carrying a gun, are sportsmen. In the north, where people lead active lives, a sportsman goes after his quarry, and, provided he bags it, has no reason to suppose that the trouble he has taken will in any degree deprive him of the good opinion of his countrymen. In the south, on the contrary, that land of indolence, he waits for the game; there, in the south, the game has to come to man, for is not man lord of the creation?

Hence the fabulous tradition of the flights of wild pigeons.

The more knowing sportsmen of Marseilles have shooting posts. These are little retreats dug in the ground, with the earth which is excavated being heaped up so as to form low walls, over which branches and dead leaves are strewn as roofing. On either side of these huts, as one may call them, stand two or three pines, near the summits of which some long bare spars stretch out like skeletons, two, as a rule, being placed horizontally, and a third vertically.

Before daybreak, every Sunday morning, the sporting gentlemen of Marseilles usually install themselves in their burrows, so arranging their branches that only their heads protrude; and even these are generally camouflaged under caps of a faded green which blend wonderfully well with the hue of the foliage. Thus the Marseillese sporstman is invisible to every eye, excepting that of the Lord.

If the sportsman is a sybarite he seats himself on a stool in his retreat, but if he is a real sportsman he simply crouches on his knees.

He is patient because he is eternal – *patiens quia aeternus.*

He waits, then, patiently.

But what does he wait for? you may ask.

Well, in normal times the Marseillese sportsman waits for thrushes, blackbirds, ortolans, fig-peckers, red-breasts, or other small birds, for his ambition never rises to quails. As for the partridge, he regards that as a phoenix; he believes, for he has heard it said, that there is but one in the world, which rises anew from its ashes, and appears from time to time, before or after great catastrophes to announce the displeasure or clemency of the Divinity. That is all. We will not speak of the hare; at

Marseilles that animal is regarded as a fabulous creature in the same way as the unicorn.

Now, as the thrushes, blackbirds, ortolans, fig-peckers and red-breasts have no motive for perching voluntarily on the pines where they are expected, the Marseillese sportsman is generally attended by a boy carrying various cages, in each of which one of the birds enumerated is imprisoned. These captives, acquired by purchase at the port, are of both sexes, the male birds being designed to call the female birds, and the females the males.

The cages are hung on the lower branches of the pines, and the captive birds call the free ones. It is expected that these unfortunates, deceived by the call, will perch on the horizontal spars; but it must be admitted that this seldom happens.

The sportsman, however, waits for it to occur. If he is skilful, he then shoots the birds; if he is clumsy he misses them. As a rule the Marseilles sportsman is clumsy, skill being the result of practice.

Méry has calculated that, since the Marseillese sportsman visits his post once a week, since one day every week a bird perches on the spars, and since for every eight birds doing so he shoots one, it follows that, allowing for the cost of land, firearms, ammunition, decoys and so forth, each of the birds thus bagged represents a sum of five-hundred or six-hundred francs. But, as an offset to this expense, whenever a Marseillese sportsman does manage to shoot a bird, he is regarded by his family as being a Nimrod.

On extraordinary occasions, for example, when a flight of wild pigeons is expected, the Marseillese sportsman simply takes a decoy pigeon to his post, and by means of a string fastens it to a perpendicular pole, around which it is compelled to fly incessantly, the pole tapering to so sharp a point that the poor bird cannot perch on it, and the string being too short to allow it to rest upon the horizontal spars. This ceaseless fluttering is expected to attract the more or less numerous flocks of pigeons which are supposed to pass over Marseilles on their way from Africa to Kamtchatka.

If any pigeons were to pass they would probably be aware of the stratagem; but the Marseillese sportsman acknowledges ingenuously that he has never seen one. This, however, does not prevent him from declaring that the alleged flights actually take place.

After four Sundays or so, the first decoy pigeon dies of exhaustion, and as the flights of wild pigeons are supposed to last three months, that is from 1 October till the end of December, the sportsman incurs the risk of three more decoys.

It must be added that, in the meantime, he bags nothing, for all other birds are frightened, scared away by the fluttering of the decoy.

As a rule the Marseillese sportsman remains from six to eight hours in his hut, that is from about four o'clock in the morning until somewhere near noon. There are even some lunatics who take their breakfast and dinners with them, and only return to their bastide in the evening to play Lotto – a game wonderfully well suited to wind up a day at a shooting post!

I asked Méry if he could introduce me to one of the sportsman I have mentioned, for they seemed to me to constitute a distinct species it would be interesting to study. Méry promised me he would avail himself of the first opportunity.

On this we separated after arranging to meet again at the theatre in the evening. After the performance we were to sup at Sybillot's restaurant. Méry left me for the purpose of ordering the repast and finding such a sportsman as I desired to meet.

I reached the theatre at the appointed time, and there, awaiting me, I found my friend Jadin, the animal-painter, with Méry and three or four others. I immediately asked Méry whether he had found me the promised sportsman.

'Oh! yes,' he answered, 'and a fine one, too!'

'You are sure he won't escape?' said I.

'Oh! he has no desire to do so. I told him that you had hunted lions in Algeria and tigers in the pampas.'

'And where is he now?'

'There, playing in the orchestra.'

'What, the third 'cello.'

'No, the fourth. Can you see him?'

'Certainly.'

'Well, that is your man.'

'Really?'

'He doesn't look like a sportsman, does he?'

'No, indeed.'

'Well, no matter, you will be able to give me your opinion of him by and by.'

Reassured by that promise, I directed my attention to the performance.

The Marseilles theatre is neither better nor worse than others. Comedy is played there rather better than at Lyons, melodrama much as one sees it at Folies-Dramatiques, and vaudeville as it is played everywhere.

That evening, it so chanced, there was a full house. A small Italian company, after performing at Nice, had crossed the Var and come to sing Rossini at Marseilles, where it was enjoying great success. As the Marseillese speak Provençal, they imagine that they understand Italian music.

Directly *Semeramide* was over – of course *Semeramide* was the opera played! – Méry made a sign to the fourth 'cellist, who responded by a similar one. Méry's gesture signified, 'We shall wait for you at Sybillot's';

and the other, 'I must take my instrument home, but I will be with you in five minutes.' Two deaf mutes could not have said more in less time.

We had scarcely reached Sybillot's when our sportsman, whose name was Louet, arrived. Méry introduced us, and we then sat down to supper. Throughout the repast Méry, Jadin, and myself strove to establish a cordial understanding. We each told some extravagant anecdotes; but Monsieur Louet never uttered a word. It appears, indeed, that nothing sharpens the appetite so much as the exercise necessitated by the horizontal movement of one hand combined with the perpendicular movement of the other. True, our musician listened to everything, and although he did not speak for fear of losing a bite, he nodded his approval of the exploits we recounted, and even gave a little grunt of satisfaction when an anecdote seemed to him particularly interesting. All the same, his prolonged silence caused me to glance reproachfully at Méry, who thereupon signed that I must allow the man time to satisfy his appetite, and I should lose nothing by waiting.

Indeed, after the dessert, Monsieur Louet gave vent to an exclamation, which seemed to signify, 'Well, I have made a good supper.' Méry at once understood that the right moment had come, and he therefore ordered a bowl of punch and some cigars. At a distance of two-hundred leagues from Paris, punch was then still regarded as the proper complement to a bachelor's supper.

Monsieur Louet threw himself back in his chair, scrutinized us all as if he now saw us for the first time, and smiled benevolently. Then with a soft sigh of satisfaction such as comes from a satisfied gourmet, he muttered, 'Yes, that was an excellent supper.'

'Try a cigar, Monsieur Louet; it is capital for one's digestion,' said Méry.

'No, thank you, my illustrious poet,' Monsieur Louet replied; 'I never smoke. But if these gentlemen will allow it, I will accept a glass of punch.'

'Allow it, Monsieur Louet! Why, it has been ordered specially for your benefit.'

'You are too kind, gentlemen.'

'Well, as you do not smoke, Monsieur Louet——'

'No, I never smoke! In my young days, gentlemen, people did not smoke. The habit was introduced into France by the Cossacks at the same time as boots. For my part, I have always worn shoes, and remained faithful to my snuff box. I am a patriot, I am!'

Thus speaking, Monsieur Louet produced a snuff box, decorated with a miniature; but only Méry, by way of humouring him, would take a pinch. 'This is excellent rapee, Monsieur Louet,' he said. 'I am sure it can be no government stuff.'

'Yes, yes, it is; only I mix it myself according to a secret recipe given me by a Cardinal when I was in Rome.'

'So you have been to Rome, then?' I enquired.

'Yes, Monsieur; I lived there for nearly twenty years.'

'Ah! Monsieur Louet,' Méry resumed, 'as you don't smoke you ought to tell these gentlemen the story of your adventure with the *chastre*.'

'What is a *chastre*?' I inquired innocently.

'Heavens!' Méry replied. 'You don't know what a *chastre* is? I say, Monsieur Louet, he doesn't know what a *chastre* is, and yet he claims to be a sportsman! Why, the *chastre* is a bird of omen, of fate, the *rara avis* of the Latin satirist.'[1]

'It is something like a blackbird,' said Monsieur Louet, 'and it is excellent when roasted.'

'Well, tell us your adventure with the *chastre*!' Méry exclaimed once more.

'Oh! I only desire to make myself agreeable to the company,' Monsieur Louet replied graciously.

'Listen, then, gentlemen!' said Méry. 'You are about to hear an account of one of the most extraordinary sporting adventures that ever befell anybody since the days of Nimrod. I myself have heard the tale a score of times, and I always renew my acquaintance with it with fresh pleasure. Come, let Monsieur Louet have a second glass of punch! There! Kindly begin, Monsieur Louet, for we are all attention.'

'You are aware, gentlemen,' said our new friend, 'that every Marseillese is a born sportsman.'

'Why, yes!' Méry interrupted, after puffing at his cigar. 'It is a physiological problem which I have never been able to explain, but none the less it is as you say. Truly, the designs of Providence are inscrutable.'

'Well,' continued Monsieur Louet, 'unluckily, or perhaps luckily, for they are regarded as scourges of humanity, there are no lions or tigers in the vicinity of Marseilles; but fortunately there are the flights of wild pigeons——'

'Eh!' Méry exclaimed, 'I told you so, my dear Dumas. They insist on it.'

'Certainly we do,' resumed Monsieur Louet, visibly nettled, 'certainly we do. And whatever you may say, the flights take place. Besides, didn't you lend me, the other day, Cooper's book, *The Pioneers*, in which the pigeon flights are described?'

'Ah! yes, in America!'

---

[1] *Chastre* is a corruption of *castorum*, the bird's Latin name being *avis castorum*.

'Well, if the pigeons fly over America why shouldn't they fly over Marseilles? The ships which sail to America from Alexandria and Constantinople call at Marseilles, don't they?'

'That is true,' said Méry, staggered by the thrust. 'I have nothing more to say. Why didn't I think of that before! Give me your hand, Monsieur Louet, I will never contradict you on that subject again.'

'Oh! discussion is allowable, Monsieur.'

'True, but I close it. Pray proceed, Monsieur Louet.'

'I was saying then, gentlemen, that if we have no lions or tigers, we have the flights of wild pigeons.'

For a moment Monsieur Louet paused, as though challenging Méry to contradict him again. But Méry only nodded assent, saying, 'That is true. They have the flights of pigeons.'

Satisfied with this acknowledgement, Monsieur Louet resumed, 'You will understand that a sportsman does not allow such an event to pass without repairing to his shooting post every morning. I say every morning, for I can fortunately dispose of my mornings, as my work only requires my presence at the theatre in the evening. Well, one morning in 1810 or 1811, when I was about five and thirty years old, gentlemen, and more active than I am now, though thank Heaven I still enjoy excellent health, I betook myself as usual to my shooting post before daybreak. A decoy-pigeon was fastened to one of my poles, and was fluttering about when, all at once, by the light of the stars, I thought I saw something settle on one of my pine trees. Unluckily there was not light enough for me to distinguish whether it was a bat or a bird. I kept perfectly still, and the creature, curiously enough, did the same, and I waited for sunrise, fully prepared for whatever might happen.

'At the first ray of light I saw that the creature was a bird. I therefore gently raised my gun to my shoulder, took careful aim, and pressed the trigger. But, most unluckily, gentlemen, I had loaded the gun the previous day and forgotten to discharge it. Consequently it hung fire. Nevertheless, from the manner in which the bird flew off I could tell it was hit. I watched it till I saw it alight; then, on glancing at my spars, I discovered to my astonishment that my shot had actually severed the string securing my decoy-pigeon, which had also flown away. Having lost it, I felt that I should also lose my time if I persisted in remaining at my post. So I decided to pursue the *chastre*, for I forgot to tell you, gentlemen, and this is important, that the bird I had fired at was a *chastre*.

'Unluckily I had no dog. At a shooting post, as you will understand, a dog is not only useless, but usually proves a dreadful nuisance. In my case, however, having none to help me, I had to beat the bushes myself in search of the bird. It had hopped some distance, and I thought it still farther away, when to my astonishment, it rose again behind me. I turned on hearing the whirr of its wings, and fired at it as it flew off. This was a waste of powder, as you will readily understand. Nevertheless, I saw some feathers fly down.'

'You saw some feathers fly down?' said Méry, interrupting.

'Yes, Monsieur, and I even picked one up and placed it in my buttonhole.'

'If you saw feathers fly down,' Méry resumed, 'the *chastre* was certainly hit.'

'That was my opinion. I had not lost sight of it, so I started in pursuit. And though it was virtually out of range I sent it a parting shot, for one can never tell what one grain of lead may do.'

'It would not suffice for a *chastre*,' said Méry, shaking his head; 'that bird dies remarkably hard.'

'True,' replied Monsieur Louet, 'mine, for instance, had been wounded by both of my first shots – I am sure of it – yet it rose again, and flew at least one-hundred yards. But as it had alighted, I swore I could overtake it, so I continued the pursuit. Ah! the rascal! It knew well what sort of customer it had to deal with! It always rose at a distance of fifty or sixty yards. Nevertheless, whether it were out of gunshot or not, I fired every time. I felt quite tigerish. If I had got hold of the impudent bird I believe I should have devoured it then and there. As a matter of fact, I was very hungry; but, luckily, as it had been my intention to remain at my shooting post all day, I had brought my breakfast and dinner in my game bag. So I ate as I ran on.'

'Excuse me!' said Méry, interrupting Monsieur Louet once more, 'just one remark. You see, my dear Dumas, the difference between the sportsman of the north and sportsman of the south. It is shown, as you will have noticed, by Monsieur Louet's own words. The sportsman of the north leaves home with his game-bag empty and brings it back full; whereas the sportsman of the south sets out with his bag full and returns with it empty. And, now pray continue your story, my dear Monsieur Louet, I have finished.' Thereupon Méry lovingly pressed his cigar stump between his lips.

'Where was I?' inquired Monsieur Louet who had lost the thread of his discourse in consequence of Méry's interruption.

'You were scouring hill and plain in pursuit of your *chastre*.'

'Oh, yes. It was vitriol, not blood, that I now had in my veins. We hot-headed men of the south become ferocious when we lose our tempers, and I had lost mine completely. That impudent *chastre* seemed a very witch. At last, leaving the villages of Cassio and La Crotal on my right, I reached the plain spreading from Ligne to St Cyr. For fifteen hours I kept up the pursuit, bearing now to the right and now to the left. If I had travelled as the crow flies I should certainly have gone farther than Toulon. As it was, my legs began to fail me. That devil of a *chastre* did not show again, and night was coming on. Barely another half-hour of daylight remained for me to overtake the confounded bird. I vowed to Notre Dame de la Garde that I would hang a *chastre* of solid silver in her chapel if I could only capture the one I was pursuing. But, possibly because I was not a mariner, she showed no sign of having even heard me. Soon the dusk fell, and at last, in my despair, I sent a final shot after the bird. It must have actually heard the lead whistle on that occasion, for it flew so far that, though I never took my eyes from it, it vanished into the twilight in the direction of the village of St Cyr. Well, I thought, there could be no question of returning to Marseilles at that hour; and so I made up my mind to sleep at St Cyr. Fortunately, it was an off-night at the theatre.

'I felt ashamed by the time I reached the inn of the Black Eagle, where I asked the landlord, an old acquaintance of mine, to let me have some supper and a bed. Then I told him my adventure, and he became anxious to know where it was I had lost sight of the *chastre*. I indicated the spot as well as I could, and, after a moment's thought, he said to me, "The bird must be in the moorland on the right hand side of the highroad."

'"Quite so!" said I. "It was there I lost it. If only the moon were up I would show you the very spot."

'"Yes, yes", said he, "that's a favourite nesting-place for *chastres*."

'"Oh, is it?"

'"Yes, and tomorrow at daybreak, if you like, we will go with my dog and start the bird."

'"Certainly I should like to. I don't mean to be beaten by a wretched pigeon. Do you think we shall find it?"

'"Certainly we shall."

'"Then I shall sleep with an easy mind. But don't go to the spot without me."

'"Why, what do you take me for?" he answered.

'Well, as I did not desire any recurrence of the mishap which had befallen me that morning, I unloaded and cleaned my gun. It was foul, gentlemen, and no wonder! If I had fired once that day I fired fifty times; and, if grains of lead only sprouted like grains of wheat, there would have been a fine crop growing between Marseilles and St Cyr! However, I placed my gun-barrel in the chimney corner to dry overnight. Then I supped, went to bed, and slept soundly till five in the morning, when the landlord roused me.

'I intended to return to Marseilles by the road I had taken the previous day, and so, to provide myself with a snack, I slipped the remains of my supper into my game-bag. I had a right to do so, gentlemen, for I had paid for the meal. Well, I slung my bag over my shoulder, went downstairs, saw to my gun, and in order to reload it, opened my powder flask. Gentlemen, it was empty!

'Fortunately, my host had a supply of ammunition, and sportsmen, as you are aware, often avail themselves of one another's powder and shot. So I accepted some of my host's powder, proved my gun, and loaded it. I ought to have noticed at the time that something was wrong by the grain of the powder, but I paid no attention to it. We set off, the landlord, myself, and Soliman. The landlord's dog was named Soliman. By the way, what is the name of yours, Monsieur Jadin?'

'Milord,' Jadin replied.

'An aristocratic name,' said Monsieur Louet, bowing, 'but although my landlord's dog was only called Soliman, all the same he was a very fine animal, for we had barely reached the moorland when he began to point.'

'"There's your *chastre*," said my landlord.

'I drew near, looked ahead on a line with his nose, and saw my *chastre*, only three steps away. I immediately took aim.

'"Why! what are you about?" cried the inn-keeper. "You will blow it to smithereens! It's murder! Besides, you may pepper my dog at the same time."

'"True," I replied, and I withdrew to a distance of ten paces, just a nice shot. Solimon seemed rooted to the ground. You might have taken him for the dog of Cephalus. The dog of Cephalus was changed to stone, as Monsieur Dumas will doubtless know.'

'No, I did not know it,' I answered smiling.

'Ah! Well, that animal, it seems, experienced that dreadful fate.'

'Poor brute!' said Méry.

'But let me return to Soliman. He was pointing marvellously well, and I feel sure he would still have been there, gentlemen, if his master had not suddenly shouted, "At it! at it!". When the dog heard those words he sprang forward, and the *chastre* flew up! I covered it, covered it as never *chastre* was covered before! I had it at the very muzzle of my gun, so to say. I fired. Alas! the inn-keeper's powder had been spoilt by exposure. I did not even touch the bird!

'"Well, friend," said my host, "if you do that *chastre* no more injury than you have done it now, it may lead you all the way to Rome!"

'"To Rome!" said I. "Well, even if I have to follow it to Rome, I'll do so. Besides, I have always wanted to see Rome, and the Pope, too. And if I choose to see him, you, at all events, won't hinder me!"

'I was furious, as you will readily understand. Had he answered me a single word I believe I should have let him taste the contents of my second barrel. But instead of arguing, he merely said, "Oh, go where you like! Goodbye, and a pleasant journey. Shall I lend you my dog? You can return him on your way back."

'That pacified me. The offer of such a fine pointer was not to be refused.

"'Then call him – Soliman, Soliman! Go and follow that gentleman."

'Everyone knows that a pointer will follow any sportsman who calls him. So Soliman followed me. We set off. That animal was instinct incarnate. He had seen the *chastre* alight again, and he went straight to the spot. I could not see the bird myself, but I was determined to show it no mercy, even if I should have to pulverize it. But my luck was out; while I was stooping and searching, that devil of a bird flew off once more. I fired at it twice, discharging both barrels, gentlemen. But the powder was bad, absolutely bad. Soliman looked at me as much as to ask, "What do you think you're doing?" I felt quite humiliated by his glance, though of course the mishap was not my fault; and I answered, just as if the animal could understand me, "That's nothing, nothing! Wait a bit, and you shall see!" You might have thought, gentlemen, that he actually did understand me. He started off once more, and ten minutes later he came to a halt. He remained as still as if he had been turned into a block of stone – a real block of stone. There was my *chastre* again! I stepped forward in a line with my dog's nose, as lightly, as gingerly, as if I had been treading on a sheet of red-hot iron; and yet that bird passed between my legs, literally between my legs! The fact is I had lost all control of myself by this time. I fired my first shot too near, the lead did not scatter at all, but passed, bullet-like, beside the bird; and the second time, as I was too far away, the lead scattered too much, and the impudent creature flew right through it.

'Then a thing happened, gentlemen, which only my deep respect for the truth induces me to mention. Soliman, that sagacious animal, gave me a scathing glance; then, coming up to me, he cocked his leg against my gaiters, and trotted off homewards! If such an outrageous insult had come from one of my fellow beings, instead of from a mere dumb quadruped, I should not have passed it over; it would have been his life or mine. As it was, the insult added fuel to my fury. I vowed that when I had killed that *chastre* I would hold his nose in it. As you may imagine, from that moment I forgot Marseilles completely. Following my bird from spot to spot, wherever it alighted, I at last got to—— Guess, gentlemen, where I got to. Why, to Hyères.

'I had never seen Hyères before, but I recognized it immediately by its orange trees. I am very fond of oranges, and I resolved to rest and eat some. Besides, I really needed some cooling refreshment, for such a journey as I had made heats the blood to boiling point. I was now fourteen leagues from Marseilles, two days' journey! But I had always wanted to visit Hyères and eat oranges from the trees. So I mentally consigned my *chastre* to a nameless place, particularly as I began to regard it as being really bewitched. I had seen it fly over the town wall and alight in a garden; but who, I ask you, could find a *chastre* in a garden? Without a dog, too? One might as well search for a needle in a bundle of hay!

'With a sigh, then, I repaired to an inn where I asked for some supper and permission to eat some oranges in the garden while the meal was being prepared. Of course, I did not mean to partake of the fruit without payment. I expected to be charged for it in my bill. The permission was granted, and as I did not feel so tired as on the previous evening – which showed me that I might soon accustom my limbs to exertion – I went into the garden at once. The month was October, the best time for oranges, and I saw something like two-hundred orange trees before me. The place suggested the Garden of the Hesperides, fortunately without the dragon. I had only to stretch out my arm to pluck an orange as large as my head, and I had begun to devour one – as a Norman devours an apple – when, all at once, I heard these notes, "Pi, pi, piiiii, pi!"'

'That is the song of the *chastre*; it is as if you heard the bird itself piping,' Méry remarked, as he helped himself to another cigar.

'I stooped,' Monsieur Louet resumed, 'and by the light of the Great Bear, I saw, midway between the Great Bear and myself, my identical *chastre*, perched on a lofty laurel bush, gentlemen, only fifteen steps away. I instinctively stretched out my hand for my gun. Alas! I had left it indoors, in the chimney corner. I could picture it standing idly there; and so, pointing at the *chastre* with my fingers, I muttered, "Yes, you might well sing; but I would make you sing a very different tune if I had my gun."'

'But why did you not go and fetch it?' I asked.

'I dared not, for fear the impudent bird should fly off to some unknown spot. I had a different plan. I thought to myself – just observe this reasoning – "I have ordered supper, it will be ready sooner or later, and then the inn-keeper will look for me. He knows that I am in the garden, and directly he arrives I shall say to him, "Friend, just be good enough to fetch my gun." You understand?'

'Hum,' said Méry, 'not bad reasoning, that.'

'Well, still remaining in a crouching posture, I continued to watch my bird. It piped, it preened its feathers, it made its toilet for the night. But I suddenly heard footsteps behind me, whereupon I waved my hand by way of enjoining silence. The inn-keeper, for it was he, drew nearer. "Look there" I whispered.

'"Ah! said he, "that is a *chastre*."

'"Hush!" I retorted, "go and fetch me my gun."

'"What for?" he inquired.

'"Fetch me my gun, I say."

'"Do you want to shoot that bird, then?" he asked.

"'Yes, indeed, it's my mortal enemy!"

"'But it can't be done.'"

"'Why not?'"

"'Because it's too late.'"

"'Too late! Why is it too late?'"

"'Because anybody firing a gun within the town after the Angelus is liable to a fine of three francs twelve sous, and two days imprisonment besides!'"

"'Never mind!' said I. 'I'll pay the fine, I'll go to prison! Bring me my gun!'"

"'So that I may be charged as your accomplice?' the inn-keeper retorted. 'No, no, wait till daylight tomorrow.'"

"'Tomorrow, idiot!' I rejoined in a louder voice than was prudent, for the bird was very near me. 'Tomorrow, why it will be gone.'"

"'Well, there are plenty of others.'"

"'But I want this one and no other! Are you aware that I have followed the damn thing all the way from Marseilles, that I mean to have it dead or alive, to pluck it, and eat it, and do whatever I choose with it? Once more, fetch me my gun!'"

"'No, I have told you already I won't. I have no wish to go to prison for your sake.'"

"'Very well, then, I will fetch it myself.'"

"'Go, if you like, but I warn you that you won't find your *chastre* when you return!'"

"'You are mean enough to scare it away!' I exclaimed, catching the inn-keeper by the collar.

"'P-r-r-r-r-o-u-u-u!' he began, but I clapped my hand to his lips.

"'Well, no, I'll tell you what,' I said. 'Fetch me my gun, and I'll give you my word of honour that I won't fire before the Angelus rings tomorrow morning. My word of honour, as an honest man! Won't that satisfy you? Fetch my gun, I'll spend the night here, and tomorrow at the last sound of the bell, bang! I'll shoot.'"

"'Pooh! A sportsman's word of honour indeed! I know a better plan.'"

"'What is that? Tell me quick. Just look at the damnable bird. It is positively laughing at me!'"

"'Well, stay here if you must. I'll send your supper out; you shall want for nothing, and if you want to sleep, you have the grass at your disposal.'"

"'Sleep! Ah! you don't know me. I shan't sleep a wink. Why, the bird might fly away while I was dreaming.'"

"'Well, tomorrow——'"

"'Tomorrow?'"

"'Yes, tomorrow morning, directly the Angelus rings, I will bring you your gun.'"

"'Inn-keeper!" exclaimed I, "you are taking an unfair advantage of me!"

"'Oh, you are free to refuse or accept."

"'And you won't fetch me my gun now, eh?'"

"'No, I won't."

"'Then go for my supper, and make as little noise as possible when you bring it."

"'Oh! you needn't worry. As the bird hasn't been scared away by all the noise we have been making, it is not likely to stir till tomorrow. Look, it is going to sleep!"

'Indeed, gentlemen, the impudent creature was tucking its head under its wing. As you may know, nearly all birds sleep in that fashion. And as this one had its head tucked under its wing, and could not see me, if it had been within my reach instead of being perched at a height of fifteen feet from the ground, I might have grasped it fast as I grasp this glass of punch. Unfortunately, it was perched too high, so I could only seat myself on the grass and await the landlord's return. He kept his word, he was an honest man, I must admit it. His wine, too, was good, if not as fine as that which you have provided this evening, gentlemen; and his supper was a comforting one. It could not be compared with tonight's, but then that has been a Belshazzar's feast, whereas his was merely an inn supper.'

We bowed in recognition of Monsieur Louet's compliment.

'But ah! how weak a creature is man!' he resumed. 'I had scarcely finished my supper in the garden when I began to feel sleepy. My eyes closed in spite of all my endeavours to keep them open. I rubbed them, I pinched my legs, I bit my little finger, but nothing availed me. I was fagged out, so I felt that I might as well sleep, and sleep I did.

'While I was in that state I began to dream that the big laurel bush on which my *chastre* was perched was sinking into the ground – as the trees do at the Marseilles theatre when there is a change of scenery, and that I was at last able to set my hand on the wretched bird. The idea thrilled me to such a degree that I gave a start and suddenly awoke.

'The bird was still in the same place, and I did not fall asleep again. I heard two o'clock, three o'clock, and then four o'clock, strike. The dawn rose. The *chastre* awoke, and once more I was on pins. When, at last, the first chimes of the Angelus fell on my ears my emotion became so great that I could scarcely breathe.

'My host kept faith with me. The Angelus was only half-tolled when he appeared, carrying my gun. Without taking my eyes from the bird, I stretched out my right arm and beckoned eagerly to the inn-keeper. But it was only at the last stroke of the bell that he gave me my weapon. And extraordinary as it may seem, gentlemen, at that same moment the *chastre* raised a faint chirp and flew away!

'I rushed to the garden wall, clung to it and scaled it. At that moment I would have climbed the highest steeple in France! The bird alighted in a hemp field. It had not yet breakfasted, gentlemen, and it hearkened to the voice of nature. Throwing a crown to the inn-keeper in payment for my supper, I leapt from the wall and ran towards the field. All my thoughts were so concentrated on the bird that I did not perceive a Rural Guard who followed me. Thus it happened that, just as I had reached the middle of the field and was about to start the bird, I felt somebody seize me by the collar. I turned – it was the Rural Guard.

'"In the name of the law!" said he, "come with me to the mayor's."

'At that identical moment the *chastre* once more took flight.

'Had I been surrounded by a regiment of grenadiers, I would have charged them all in pursuit of my bird! I knocked the Rural Guard down without the slightest compunction, as if he had been a mere scarecrow, and then rushed from that inhospitable spot. Fortunately the *chastre* had flown a long distance, so that I was soon far away from my antagonist. When I reached the place where the bird had alighted, I was so breathless, I shook with such intense emotion, that I could not even take aim. But, as I said to the *chastre*, "A game postponed is not necessarily lost."

'I continued the pursuit; I tramped and tramped all day, gentlemen, and this time, unfortunately, my game-bag was empty. I was reduced, therefore, to eating wild fruit, and drinking such water as the brooks supplied. The perspiration streamed from my forehead; I panted; I must have looked hideous. At last I reached a river-bed which was dry.'

'It was the Var,' Méry interrupted.

'You are right, Monsieur, it was the Var, with a dry bed. I crossed it, never imagining that I was setting foot on a foreign soil. But that was of no account. I could see my *chastre* hopping along some two-hundred paces in advance of me, and now there was not a single blade of grass in which it could hide. I drew near to it with wolfish stealth, aiming at it every dozen paces. But it still kept beyond gunshot, when, all at once, a hawk, which had been circling overhead, dropped like a stone, seized my *chastre* and disappeared with it in its clutches!

'I was overwhelmed, gentlemen. And now for the first time I began to feel a hundred pains. My body was covered with injuries I had received while scrambling through bushes and briars. Besides, the wild-fruit diet, with which I had tried to lull my appetite, did not agree with me at all. I sank down by the roadside, utterly overcome.

'At last a peasant passed. "My friend," I said to him, "is there any town or village or shelter of any kind in the vicinity?"

'"*Gnor, si*," he answered in the Italian of the Riviera, "*cé la citta di Nizza un miglia avanti* – Yes sir, the town of Nice lies a mile ahead."

'I was in Italy, gentlemen, and at that time I knew scarcely a word of the language. And all this had befallen me on account of a cursed *chastre*.'

* * *

'There was only one course for me to take. I rose as best I could, using my gun as a staff, and I spent an hour and a half in walking the mile which separated me from Nice. Previously I had been sustained by hope, and now, hope having forsaken me, I realized how weak and tired I was.

'At last I reached the town, and asked the first person I met to direct me to a good inn, for, as you will understand, I was in dire need of food and drink. Luckily, the person to whom I addressed myself spoke the purest French, and recommended me to go to the York Hotel. It was then the best in the town.

'I ordered a room for one, and supper for four.

'"You are doubtless expecting three friends, Monsieur," said the waiter.

'"Never mind, order the supper," I answered, and the man left me to do so.

'I then slipped my hand into my pocket to ascertain how large an amount I could afford to spend on my meal, for I felt I might never be able to eat enough to satisfy my hunger. Ah! gentlemen, a cold perspiration burst from every pore of my skin as I drew my hand out again.

'There was a hole in my pocket!

'It was the early part of October, and I had recently received my salary. On the morning of my departure from Marseilles I had slipped several 5-franc pieces into my pocket, and it was their weight and friction which had caused the hole. They were now strewn, like all my ammunition, along the road from Hyères to Nice. I searched every pocket, gentlemen, but I could not find a copper. I had not even enough money to pay my passage across the Styx.

'Thoughts of the supper for four which I had just ordered suddenly flashed upon me. I could feel my hair rise on end. I rushed at the bell-rope, and tugged at it. The waiter, who must have thought somebody was murdering me, hastened in.

'"Waiter!" said I, "waiter! have you ordered the supper?"

'"Yes, Monsieur."

'"Then stop it – stop it at once!"

'"But your friends, Monsieur?"

'"They have just called to me through the window that they are not hungry."

'"But that won't prevent you from supping, Monsieur, will it?"

'"Can't you understand," I retorted impatiently, "that if my friends have no appetite, I have none either."

'"No doubt you dined very late, Monsieur," said the man.

'"Very late."

'"And you require nothing?"

'"I require to be left alone!"

'My brief replies were ejaculated in a tone which alarmed the waiter. He hurried away, and I heard him saying to a companion, who asked him who I was, "I don't know, but he must be some English Milord, for he is terribly arrogant."

'A lord, indeed! You know what I am, gentlemen, and you will agree with me that this waiter cannot have been a physiognomist.

'My position was by no means pleasant. My garments were in shreds. I had only my gun left; but what price could I hope to get for my gun? In all probability only a small one. True, I had a diamond ring, but it had been given me by a person whom I had deeply loved, and I would rather have starved to death than have parted with it. Then I called to mind the proverb, "He who sleeps dines"; and presuming that it would apply to supper as well as to the earlier meal, I plunged between the bedclothes. Incredible as it may seem, gentlemen, I was so desperately tired that in spite of my hunger and anxiety I fell asleep.

'But I awoke with a wolfish appetite. That expression, as you know, is used not only in reference to animals, but also in reference to the human species when hunger reaches its most violent stage.

'I sat up in bed to decide what I should do, and I was twiddling my thumbs with increasing nervousness when, all at once, in a corner of my room, I perceived a violoncello. I uttered a cry of joy.

'You may ask, gentlemen, what there is in common between a 'cello and a man who has neither dined nor supped, except it be that a void exists in both. Well, in my case there was this – that instrument was like a familiar face in a foreign clime. It was indeed a friend, gentlemen; for when a man has hugged a 'cello night after night for ten long years, a bond exists between them. And for my part I have often noticed that nothing brightens my ideas so much as the music of a 'cello. Are you a musician, Monsieur Dumas?'

'Alas! no, Monsieur,' I answered.

'But you are fond of music.'

'To be honest with you, Monsieur Louet, I can only say with a certain gentleman – I forget his name – I am not afraid of music!'

At this, Méry shrugged his shoulders as a sign of profound contempt, and gave me a withering glance.

'It is a case of defective organism,' exclaimed Monsieur Louet, in a conciliatory spirit, fearing that the general good feeling of our party might be disturbed. 'The gentleman is more to be pitied than blamed. He is deficient in the fifth sense. I pity you, Monsieur.'

'Well, Monsieur Louet,' said Méry, 'I'm sure that as soon as you had the 'cello between your legs, ideas came to you by scores, by thousands. You had too many, eh?'

'No, Monsieur, no; instead of ideas it was the hotel servants who hastened to my room. While I was playing I imparted some expression of my feelings to the instrument. I drew heart-rending groans from its depths – all my yearnings for my native spot, all the anguish of the void within me also. It was expressive music of the highest order; and as you, gentlemen, must be aware, the natives of the country where I found myself are not like Monsieur Dumas. They are passionately fond of music. Thus I heard people trooping in the passage outside my room. From time to time a murmur of approval reached my ears. There was even clapping. At length the door opened and the hotel-keeper entered. After a last stroke of the bow – a stroke of genius, you understand – I turned towards him. With a 'cello in my grasp, I was conscious of my superiority over this man.

'"I beg Monsieur's pardon for thus intruding on him," said the landlord, "but Monsieur himself is the cause of it."

'"Well, you are master here," I replied. "You are in your own house."

'I must here observe that I was clad for the moment much after the fashion of Orpheus, that is in a mere tunic, otherwise my shirt.

'"Monsieur appears to be a distinguished instrumentalist," the landlord continued.

'"I have refused the post of first 'cello at the Paris opera house," I answered. That was not scrupulously accurate, I must admit, but I was on foreign soil, remember, and it was my duty to uphold the dignity of France.

'"Yet that must be a good appointment, Monsieur," said the hotel-keeper.

'"Ten-thousand francs a year and my board – cutlets and Bordeaux claret for breakfast every morning." The mention of those two items of sustenance came to my lips instinctively. "And I declined all that," I added, "for the love of art, for the sake of visiting Italy, the land of the sublime Paesiello and the divine Cimarosa."

'I was flattering the man.

'"And does not Monsieur intend to make a stay in our town?" he inquired.

'"Why should I?"

'"Why, to give a musical performance."

'That remark, gentlemen, was like a ray of celestial light.

'"A performance!" I retorted disdainfully. "Do you think a town like Nice would remunerate me sufficiently?"

"'Why, Monsieur, at this very moment, we are full of consumptive English people, who have come to spend the winter at Nice. I myself have fifteen of them here at the York Hotel.'

"'Well, it is the best hotel in Nice,' I answered, still flattering the man. "They say above all that its table is excellent.'

"'I hope that Monsieur will judge of that himself before leaving.' said he.

"'I can hardly promise as yet——'

"'It is not for me to advise Monsieur, but I am convinced that if he would only give us a soirée his time would not be wasted.'

"'And what do you think,' I inquired in an offhand manner, "would be the return of such a soirée?'

"'If Monsieur would allow me to make the announcements and distribute the tickets, I would guarantee him a hundred crowns.'

"'A hundred crowns!' I exclaimed.

"'Oh! I am aware that is not much, Monsieur, but Nice is not Paris or Rome.'

"'It is a charming town!' I said, still flattering the man, for this ingratiated me with him, "and taking its merits into consideration, well, yes, if I could be sure that I should be put to no trouble with respect to details, but merely have to take my 'cello and charm the audience, receiving in return a hundred crowns——'

"'I guarantee you that amount, Monsieur.'

"'And my board also, as at the Paris opera house?'

"'And your board also.'

"'Very well then, you may announce me, bill me.'

"'Your name, Monsieur, if you please.'

"'Monsieur Louet, who has arrived at Nice from Marseilles, in pursuit of a *chastre*.'

"'Is it quite necessary to insert that in the bill?'

"'Absolutely necessary, Monsieur, for I am in shooting costume, and without such an explanation the respectable people of Nice might think me disrespectful, though I give you my word of honour that disrespect is quite foreign to my nature.'

"'As you wish, Monsieur. And pray what will you play?'

"'Announce nothing, Monsieur. Send for all the scores at the theatre. I know every one of them, and will play them compositions of the highest order as the audience may select. That will flatter the English, for as you are aware, those islanders pride themselves on their good taste.'

"'Then it is agreed, Monsieur,' the hotel-keeper resumed. "I will guarantee you a hundred crowns and board you. Your breakfast shall be brought up at once.'

"'Remember, Monsieur,' said I, "that by this token I shall judge how you are in the habit of keeping your engagements.'

"'Be easy," he rejoined, and as he withdrew, I heard him call to his subordinates, "A first-class breakfast for Number Four! Sharp!"

'Gentlemen, I looked at the number on my door, it was four, none other. I could scarcely contain myself for joy. Taking the 'cello in my arms I danced a saraband. Just as I was reconducting my partner to her place, the waiters came in with the breakfast. It really was a first-class one; and if you should go to Nice, gentlemen, take my advice, stay at the York Hotel. Should the same man keep it now, which is quite possible, for when I knew him he was of much the same age as myself, I shall be glad to hear your opinion of him.

'I must confess that I sat down to breakfast with a feeling of intense satisfaction. For exactly eight-and-twenty hours I had not tasted food. I was drinking a cup of coffee, when the hotel-keeper returned.

"'Are you satisfied, Monsieur?" he inquired.

"'Delighted!"

"'Well, I have done everything that can be done. There can be no drawing back now. The bills announcing you are already out."

"'I will honour them, never fear! But can you tell me how I can get back to Marseilles? I should like to return tomorrow."

"'Well, there is a fine brig in the harbour, which will sail for Toulon tomorrow. The Captain is a friend of mine, a genuine old sea dog."

"'Indeed! I am not acquainted with Toulon, and should rather like to visit it."

"'Then profit by this opportunity."

"'But the fact is I don't like the sea" – that is true, gentlemen, in that respect I resemble Monsieur Méry.

"'Oh! just now the sea is as smooth as glass," said the hotel-keeper.

"'And how long does the passage take?" I asked.

"'Six hours at the utmost."

"'Oh!, that's a mere bagatelle. I will sail in the brig."

'The concert took place at the appointed time. Modesty will not allow me to say more about it. I received the hundred crowns in full; and the next day, having generously distributed a fantasia on the 'cello among the waiters, by way of gratuity, I embarked on the good brig, *Our Lady of Sorrow*, Captain Garnier commanding.

★ ★ ★

'What I had foreseen, gentlemen, took place,' resumed Monsieur Louet. 'I had scarcely set foot on deck when I felt it would soon be all up with me if I did not immediately retire to my cabin.

'After a couple of hours had passed, just as I was feeling a little better, I heard a great commotion on the deck above. Then a drum beat, and I thought it might be a signal for breakfast.

"'My friend,' I said to a sailor whom I saw carrying an armful of cutlasses, "what does that drum mean?"

"'It means that the English are coming, my good fellow,' replied the seaman with the frank familiarity which characterizes his profession.

"'The English! The English!' said I, "Oh! they are all right. I am indebted to them for three-quarters of the money I took last night.'

"'Well, they may take it all back this morning,' replied the man. And with these words he walked towards the companion-way.

'Behind him came another carrying an armful of pikes; then another with a bundle of hatchets. At the sight of them I began to suspect that something strange was occurring.

'The hubbub grew, increasing my apprehensions in proportion; but suddenly I heard somebody call down the hatchway, "Antony! bring me my pipe!"

"'Yes, Captain!' was the answer.

'A moment afterwards I saw a cabin-boy carrying the Captain's pipe. I caught him by the collar, for his tender years warranted that familiarity on my part, and I said to him, "Tell me, my young friend, what is that rumpus? Are they having breakfast up above?"

"'Ay, they're having breakfast allright!' he replied. "What with feasting on lead and steel some of them are likely to be troubled with indigestion. But I must be off. The Captain is waiting for his pipe."

"'Oh, if he wants his pipe, there can't be much danger,' said I.

"'On the contrary, he only asks for it when things are getting warm.'

"'What is warming them?"

"'Why a stew big enough for everybody. Go on deck and you'll see for yourself.'

'I understood that my best course was to follow the lad's advice. But this was not so easy on account of the manner in which the vessel rolled. However, by clinging to partitions, I managed to reach the companion way, and on grasping the rail tightly I felt comparatively at ease. Popping my head through the hatchway with all due precaution, I perceived the Captain seated on a chest, four steps away. He was quietly smoking.

"'Good morning, Captain,' I said with the most amiable smile I could contrive. "It appears that there is something fresh on board."

"'Oh! is that you, Monsieur Louet?' he responded. The worthy man knew that my name was Louet.

"'Yes,' I answered. "I have been rather ill as you may perceive, but I feel better now.'

"'Well, Monsieur Louet, have you ever seen a naval action?' asked the Captain.

"'Never, Monsieur!'

"'Would you like to see one?"

"'Well, Monsieur, I must confess that I should prefer to see something else.'"

"'I am sorry to hear that, because if you wished to see one – a first-class one – you might be humoured almost immediately.'"

"'Eh!'" I exclaimed, turning pale in spite of myself. It is known, gentlemen, that pallor comes over one quite independently of one's will. "Eh! You surely don't mean to say that we are about to witness a naval action! You must be joking, Captain!"

"'Oh! it's a joke, is it? Well, climb another couple of steps and look around you. There! Can you see now?'"

"'Yes, Captain.'"

"'And pray what do you see?'"

"'I see three fine vessels yonder.'"

"'Count again!'"

"'I see four.'"

"'Have another try!'"

"'Five! Six!'"

"'Indeed!'"

"'Yes, there are really six.'"

"'Do you know anything about flags?'"

"'Very little.'"

"'Never mind, look at the flag which the largest ship is flying from her gaff, just as we fly our tricolour. What can you see on that flag?'"

"'I know very little about heraldry, but it seems to me that I can distinguish a harp——'"

"'Well, that is the harp of Ireland. In another five minutes we shall hear a twang from it.'"

"'But, Captain,'" I exclaimed, "Captain, they are still a long way off, and it seems to me that if you were to spread all that canvas which is now hanging idle, you might easily give them the slip. I know I should make a bolt for it if I were in your place. You will excuse me – won't you? – but that is my opinion as fourth 'cello of the theatre of Marseilles; and I should be glad if your views were the same. Of course, if I were a sailor, my opinion might be different——'"

"'If a man, instead of a 'cellist, had spoken to me as you have just spoken,'" replied the Captain, "there would be trouble between us. Please understand that Captain Garnier never runs away. He fights till his ship is crippled. Then he awaits the boarders, and when they swarm over his deck, he goes down to the gun room with his pipe, puts it to a keg of powder, and blows them to kingdom come!"

"'Come, Captain, don't joke like that!'"

"'I never joke, Monsieur Louet, when once 'clear for action!' has sounded.'"

"'But Captain, Captain, by all the Rights of Man, it is your duty to set me on shore at once! Besides, I prefer to go home on foot. That's how I travelled to Nice, and I'll find my way to Marseilles in the same fashion.'

"'Shall I give you some advice, Monsieur Louet?' asked the Captain, laying his pipe beside him.

"'Give it by all means,' I answered. "Advice is always welcomed by a sensible man.'

'I was pleased, you see, to give him a little lesson in an indirect manner.

"'Well, Monsieur Louet,' he resumed, "my advice to you is to go to bed. You have just come from your cabin, have you not? Then go back to it.'

"'But one last question, Captain——'

"'What is it?'

"'Have we no chance of safety at all? I ask you this as a married man, with wife and family.'

'I said that, in the hope of arousing him to some compassion. As a matter of fact I was a bachelor.

'The Captain seemed to soften, and I congratulated myself on my ruse. "Listen, Monsieur Louet," said he, "I can understand that the position is unpleasant for a man who does not belong to my calling. Yes, there is a chance.'

"'What is it, Captain?' I cried. "What is it? If I can be of the slightest use to you, I am entirely at your service.'

"'Do you see that black cloud yonder, in the south-west?'

"'I see it as plainly as I see you, Monsieur.'

"'It seems to promise nothing more than a little squall. But just go below and pray for it to turn into a tempest.'

"'A tempest, Captain! But we might be wrecked if there should be a tempest!'

"'Well, that is the best thing that can happen to us,' said Captain Garnier.

'Then he took up his pipe again; but I noticed with satisfaction that it had gone out.

"'Antony!' he cried, "Antony! Where have you got to, you wretched sprat!'

"'Here I am, Captain!' replied the cabin-boy, popping his head through the hatchway.

"'Go and light my pipe again, for unless I'm much mistaken the ball is about to begin.'

'At this moment a little white cloud appeared on the starboard side of the vessel which was nearest to us, and was followed by a deep boom, such as comes from a big drum at a theatre. I saw a portion of the brig's bulwarks fly into splinters; and a gunner, who had climbed up to have a better look, fell against my shoulder.

"'Here! be careful, my friend!" I said to him. "You may think it amusing to lark like that, but it isn't."

'As he would not move, I gave him a push, and he fell upon the deck. Then, on looking at him more attentively, I perceived that the poor devil had no head.

'The sight produced such a terrible effect on my nerves, gentlemen, that five minutes later I was down in the brig's hold. How long I remained there I cannot say, but I heard such a blaring of brass instruments as, despite all my experience of orchestras, I had never heard before. And, after that pandemonium, there came such deep bass music that I really began to think the overture to the end of the world was being played. I was not at all happy, gentlemen, no, I was not. I must admit it.

'At last, after losing all count of time, I found that things were becoming quieter. Nevertheless, I remained motionless in my shelter for another full hour. Then, as all the bustle had quite ceased, I went above again, and found myself between decks. Everything was quiet there except for the moans of a few wounded men. So I mustered courage and ascended to the quarter-deck. Gentlemen, you will hardly believe it, but we were in port!

"'Well," said Captain Garnier, slapping me on the shoulder, "here we are, Monsieur Louet!"

"'Yes, indeed," I replied, "we seem to be in safety now."

"'Thanks to the storm which I foresaw. The English had so much to do to provide for their own safety that they had no time to attend to us. In such a way we literally passed between their legs."

"'As between those of the Colossus of Rhodes," said I. You know, gentlemen, that according to the historians, ships were once base enough to pass between the legs of that colossus.

"'And," I added to the Captain, "that is probably the Isle of St Marguerite yonder?"

"'What?"

"'I say", and as I spoke I pointed to an island on the horizon, "I say that is probably the Isle of St Marguerite, where the Man in the Iron Mask was imprisoned for a time."

"'That!" exclaimed the Captain.

"'Yes, that!"

"'That is the island of Elba."

"'Elba!" I cried. "In that case my knowledge of geography must be very defective, for I did not imagine that the island of Elba was so near to Toulon."

"'Where do you see Toulon?'"

"'Why this town is Toulon, isn't it? Isn't this port that of Toulon? When we started, Captain, didn't you tell me that we were bound for Toulon?'"

"'My dear Monsieur Louet, you know the proverb, Man proposes——'"

"'And God disposes,' I rejoined. "Yes, Monsieur, I know that proverb; it is a very philosophical one.'"

"'And a very truthful one,' said the Captain, "for Providence has disposed of us.'"

"'But where are we?' I cried.

"'At Piombino.'"

"'Piombino!' I exclaimed. "Why, how dreadful! If this kind of thing continues I shall return to Marseilles by way of the Sandwich Islands where Captain Cook was killed.'"

"'Well, you are certainly not on the way to Marseilles now.'"

"'Indeed, I am a long way off.'"

"'But what about me then? I come from Brittany.'"

"'And how are we to get back?'"

"'To Brittany?'"

"'No, to Marseilles.'"

"'Well, my dear Monsieur Louet, you can sail back in my ship.'"

"'Thank you, but I have had enough of it.'"

"'In that case you may travel by land, by the coach.'"

"'Yes, I much prefer to travel by land.'"

"'Well, then, my dear Monsieur Louet, I will have you put on shore.'"

"'You will oblige me by doing so, Captain,' I replied.

'Captain Garnier immediately hailed a boat. As you are aware, I was not burdened with luggage, I had only my gun and my game-bag to carry. I took leave of the Captain, wishing him a safe return, and then prepared to descend the ladder.

'But at that moment he called me again. "What is it, Monsieur?" I asked.

'He seemed embarrassed. "You know, my dear Monsieur Louet," he began, "that compatriots ought not to stand on ceremony with one another."

"'I am aware of that, Monsieur.'"

"'Then you understand?'"

"'Yes, Monsieur, I understand,' I replied, "though I don't quite know what you are driving at. You mean——'"

"'I mean——' repeated the Captain.

"'You mean——' said I once more.

"'Well, hang it! I mean that if you are in want of money, my purse is at your service. There, it's said now.'"

'Gentlemen, the manner in which he made me that offer brought tears to my eyes.

"'Thank you, Captain," I said, offering him my hand, "but I am well off."

"'Oh! as a rule . . . musicians——"

"'I have a hundred crowns in this handkerchief, Captain."

"'A hundred crowns! Oh! in that case you have enough to carry you to the end of the world!"

"'I don't wish to go so far, Captain; I shall be quite content to remain at Marseilles, once I get there."

"'Then a pleasant journey to you," said he. "Don't forget me in your prayers."

"'If I live a hundred years, Captain, I shall never forget you," I answered.

"'Goodbye, Monsieur Louet."

"'Goodbye, Captain Garnier."

'I took my seat in the boat, and the Captain crossed the brig's deck to watch me. "Go to the 'French Hussar,' 'L'Ussero Francese'," he called, "That is the best hotel."

'Those were the last words he spoke to me, gentlemen. I can see him now, poor man, leaning against the bulwarks, and smoking a cigar, for he reserved his pipe for great occasions. Ah! poor Captain!'

Monsieur Louet paused.

'What happened to him then?' I asked.

'What happened to him, Monsieur? Well, three months later he was cut in half by a shot from an English 36 pounder.'

We naturally respected Monsieur Louet's grief, and Méry, by way of doing all he could to alleviate it, replenished his glass with punch for the third time.

'Gentlemen,' said Monsieur Louet, raising his arm level with his eyes, 'I will give you a toast to which none can take objection: "To the memory of the brave Captain Garnier!"'

We honoured the toast, and Monsieur Louet then resumed his story.

* * *

'I went straight to the Hotel of the French Hussar, which I found easily enough, for it faced the harbour. I at once ordered dinner, being very hungry. Indeed, as you must have observed, gentlemen, for some time now, I had made only one meal every four-and-twenty hours. After dinner I sent for a vetturino, a kind of petty job-master. It was evident that my manager at Marseilles, not knowing what had become of me, must be feeling very anxious, and I was therefore eager to get back. I found that my absence had already lasted a week, during which, it is true, I had not exactly idled away my time, though, on the other hand, I had certainly not done what I had intended.

'I summoned, in succession, three of those Italian job-masters, without being able to arrive at any understanding with them, for they did not speak my mother-tongue. At last there came a fourth man, who pretended he could speak every language, whereas he could really speak none – that is to say, intelligibly. Nevertheless, by means of his medley of French, English and Italian we managed to exchange ideas. His suggestion was that I should pay him thirty francs to be taken to Florence, where, he assured me, I should find a thousand opportunities for returning to Marseilles. As I was very desirous of seeing Florence I agreed to give him the thirty francs. Before he departed, he told me that two of his passengers, one of whom was a Frenchman like myself, had stipulated that the journey should be made by way of Grosseto and Siena, as they wished to pass through the mountains. I replied that I had no objections to the mountains, but that the sea was another matter. To this he replied that I should be turning my back to the sea throughout the journey, and with that assurance I was satisfied.

'We were to start the same afternoon, and sleep at Scarlino. At two o'clock the coach arrived outside the hotel. Four travellers were already seated in it, and the driver had called for me and my compatriot, who was staying at the same place as myself. I was waiting, in readiness, on the threshold – for as you are aware I had no great preparations to make, having still only the same light luggage, my gun and my game-bag – when I heard the driver call "Monsieur Ernest". It quite delighted me to hear a French name.

'Monsieur Ernest came out. He was a handsome officer of Hussars between six and eight and twenty years of age. Leaving the insignia of his rank out of count, he looked exactly like the Hussar on the hotel signboard. He slipped a brace of pistols into the pocket of the coach, then seated himself beside me.

'It did not take me long to observe that Monsieur Ernest had something preying on his mind. I did not know him well enough to ask what it might be, but, at all events, I was desirous of enlivening him by conversation.

'"Monsieur is French?" I said to him.

'"Yes, Monsieur," he replied.

'"Monsieur is in the army?" I continued.

'But this time he merely shrugged, though my question certainly was not indiscreet, for he was in full uniform. I concluded, however, that he did not desire to converse, and so I remained silent. As for the other travellers, they spoke Italian. As I have already told you, gentlemen, I did not then understand that language, so you will not be surprised to hear that I refrained from joining in the conversation.

'In this way, without exchanging a word, we reached a very bad inn at Scarlino, and spent a horrible night, for the place swarmed with vermin. I was at last just on the point of falling asleep, about three o'clock in the morning, when the coach driver entered my room and warned me that it was time to get up. It seems that in Italy it is the rule for the coaches to start at unreasonable hours.

'Carrying my gun and bag, I was about to take the seat I had occupied the previous day, when the driver stopped me, saying something of which I could make neither head nor tail.

'"What do you mean?" I asked him.

'"He wishes to know if your gun is loaded," said Monsieur Ernest.

'"Your servant, Monsieur!" I replied, turning to the young officer. "May I inquire if you have slept well?"

'"Perfectly well," he answered.

'"Then you are not hard to please," said I. "For my part——"

'But at this moment the other travellers exclaimed in chorus, "*Andiamo, andiamo* – let us be off, let us be off!" while the driver continued to address me on the subject of my gun.

'I begged the young officer to act as my interpreter, and thereupon ascertained that the man wished me to unload my gun, for fear, no doubt, of an accident.

'"Ah! He is right," I said. "I will unload it."

'"Pray do nothing of the kind," Monsieur Ernest retorted. "Leave your gun as it is. If we should be stopped by robbers we should at least be able to defend ourselves with your gun and my pistols."

'"Robbers, Monsieur!" I exclaimed. "Can there be any robbers on this road?"

'"Why, there are robbers everywhere in Italy," said he.

'"Driver!" I called, "driver! Why did you not warn me that there were robbers on this road?"

'"*Avanti! avanti!*" the other passengers now began to call.

'"Come, jump in," said Monsieur Ernest. "Our fellow passengers are getting impatient, and we certainly shall not reach Siena before midnight."

'"Wait until I unload my gun," I answered.

'"No, no!" said the officer to me. "Leave it as it is, and jump in."

'"Excuse me, Monsieur," I replied, "but I share the driver's opinion. If we should by chance meet any robbers, I should not like them to suspect me of evil intentions towards them——"

'"In other words you are afraid?"

"'I do not deny it, Monsieur. I am not a soldier like you. I play the 'cello at the Theatre of Marseilles – Monsieur Louet, fourth 'cello at your service," I added with a bow.

"'Ah! you are 'cellist at the Marseilles Theatre! Then you must have known a charming danseuse who was there three or four years ago."

"'I have known many charming danseuses, Monsieur," said I, "for my seat in the orchestra is an excellent one for making their acquaintance. Is it indiscreet to ask the name of the one to whom you refer?"

"'Mademoiselle Zéphirine."

"'Ah, yes, Monsieur, I knew her well. She quitted our city for Italy. She was an extremely light young woman——"

"'Eh!" exclaimed Monsieur Ernest.

"'I apply the term physically, only physically," said I, "and in the case of a dancer it is a term of praise" – here I assumed my most amiable expression – "or else I know nothing about it."

"'That is true!"

'At this moment the other passengers again called from the coach; I gathered that they wished to know whether we were likely to start that day or not.

"'One moment, gentlemen," I said to them, "I am just going a short distance to discharge my gun, for fear lest the horses should be frightened by the double report."

'But the driver took the weapon from my hands, explaining that he would deposit it in the hood.

"'Dear me!" I said. "I never thought of that. Here it is, my good man. Take care of it, it is an excellent weapon."

"'Now, will you get in?" said Monsieur Ernest again.

"'Here I am, Monsieur, here I am!"

'I got into the coach, the driver shut the door, climbed into his hood, and we started.

"'You were saying," I resumed, turning to Monsieur Ernest in delight at having discovered a subject of conversation which seemed to interest him, "You were saying that Mademoiselle Zéphirine——"

"'You are mistaken," Monsieur Ernest interrupted. "I was saying nothing at all."

'By this I perceived that his desire for a chat was over, and I became silent.

'Seldom, gentlemen, have I made a more tiresome journey than that, or one over worse roads. Our driver seemed determined to avoid all towns and villages. You might have thought we were travelling through uncivilized country. We halted to dine at a wretched hut, where we ate an omelette made of eggs which were nearly hatched, and where our driver entered into conversation with several evil-looking fellows, an occurrence which gave me some suspicions. I wished to impart them to my travelling companions, but I could not speak Italian; and, as for Monsieur Ernest, the manner in which he had received my previous advances did not encourage me to address him again.

'We resumed our journey, gentlemen, but the road, instead of improving, became even viler. It would be no exaggeration to say that we travelled through desert-like solitudes. Eventually we reached a kind of pass, with mountains upon one side, and a torrent on the other. To make us feel more uncomfortable, night was now approaching. None of us spoke, not even the Italians, and we only heard the driver swearing occasionally at his horses. At last I asked if we were still very far from Siena, and learnt that we were about half-way.

'It then occurred to me that if I could only sleep, the journey would appear very much shorter. I therefore made myself as comfortable as I could in my corner, and closed my eyes as an inducement to slumber. I even tried to snore, but found that the effort of doing so kept me awake, and therefore abandoned that method as inefficacious.

'It is said, however, "where there's a will there's a way", and the truth of that axiom was exemplified in my case. After an hour's strenuous effort I fell into that semi-somnolent state in which a man retains some perception of his surroundings, though the command of his faculties is gone. How long I remained in that state, I cannot say; but, all at once, it seemed to me that the coach had stopped.

'A great deal of bustle followed. I tried to wake up, but could not do so. In fact, I had mesmerized myself. All at once, however, I heard two pistol-shots. That was more than I could bear, so I opened my eyes. And then what did I see, pointed at my breast, gentlemen? My own gun! Ah! how I repented that I had not unloaded it!

'We had been stopped by a band of brigands, who were shouting at the top of their voices, "*Faccia in terra*! Face to the ground." I sprang out of the coach immediately, and yet not fast enough to please the scoundrels, for one of them, with the butt end of my own gun, struck me a blow on the nape of the neck – the very blow, gentlemen, with which one kills a rabbit! Luckily, for me, my brain was uninjured, though I fell to the ground, hurting my nose as I did so. And I saw that all my travelling companions were prostrate like myself, that is with the exception of Monsieur Ernest, who was struggling like a demon. But even he, at last, was obliged to surrender.

'Gentlemen, those brigands searched all my garments, even my flannel undervest – excuse my mentioning it, but I wear flannel, because it is so good for the health. Every one of my hundred crowns was taken from me! When, in the hope of saving my diamond ring, I turned the stone round, I realized that it unfortunately lacked the power of the ring of

Gyges. This, you will remember, became invisible, as soon as the stone of his ring was turned. But the brigands still saw me and my ring also. They took it from me without ceremony.

'They spent nearly an hour searching and researching us in this horrid manner; and afterwards a man, who appeared to be their leader, suddenly inquired, "Is anyone of these gentlemen a musician?"

'The question seemed to me a very strange one, and I did not think it by any means an appropriate moment to declare my profession. But the man repeated, "Well, cannot you hear me? I ask if any of you gentlemen can play any musical instrument."

'"Why of course," came the reply in a voice which I recognized as that of Monsieur Ernest, "there is Monsieur Louet who plays the 'cello."

'At that moment I wished I had been a hundred feet under ground, and I remained as still as if I were quite dead.

'"Which of you is Monsieur Louet?" asked the brigand leader. "Is it you?"

'I heard steps approaching, and felt a hand on the collar of my shooting-jacket. In a trice I was pulled up and set upon my feet.

'"In heaven's name, what do you want of me, what do you want of me?" I gasped.

'"Why," replied the bandit-leader (I forgot to mention that he spoke French), "why, only something which you ought to take as a very great compliment. For a week past, we have been seeking a musician without finding one, and the Captain has quite lost his temper over it. But he will be pleased now!"

'"What! is it in order to take me to your Captain that you wish to know if I play any instrument?" I stammered.

'"Of course it is."

'"And you are going to separate me from my companions?"

'"Why, what could we do with them? They are not musicians," said the man.

'"Gentlemen!" I cried imploringly, "Help me! Surely you will not suffer me to be carried off like this!"

'"Those gentlemen," replied the chief brigand, "will be kind enough to remain as they are, without stirring, for another quarter of an hour. They may then resume their journey. As for the young officer", and here the man turned to four of his subordinates, who were holding Monsieur Ernest, "bind him to a tree. In a quarter of an hour the driver may set him at liberty. You hear, driver! If you release him before a quarter of an hour has elapsed you will have to deal with me, the Picard!"

'The driver gave a kind of groan, which might have been taken as implying that he would obey the injunction. For my part, my strength seemed to have evaporated. A mere child might have mastered me. Thus all was easy for the two stout fellows who held me by the collar.

'"Well, let us be off!" the brigand leader resumed. "Treat the musician with every consideration. If he resists, you need only push him – you know how."

'I was curious to ascertain in what manner they would push me if I offered resistance, and so, in spite of my weakness, I did resist. Gentlemen, I then received such a kick that everything danced before me! My curiosity was quite satisfied.

'The brigands took the road to the mountains, whose crests rose darkly against the sky. After walking some five-hundred paces we crossed a torrent, then entered and threaded a forest of pine trees. On emerging from it, we perceived a light.

'We went towards this light, which shone from the window of a small inn, facing a cross-road. At some fifty paces from the inn, we halted, one man going forward, alone, to reconnoitre. A signal he made by clapping his hands three times doubtless indicated to the Picard that we might approach, for our march was at once resumed, and the bandits began to sing, which they had not done since quitting the highway.

'When I set foot on the threshold of that inn, gentlemen, I heard such an uproar that I thought Satan was keeping festival there.

'"*Ove sta, il Capitano?*" asked the Picard on entering, and I understood that he wished to know where the Captain was.

'"*Al primo piano,*" the inn-keeper answered.

'"What!" thought I, "there is a first piano, and the Captain is playing it. This man has a passion for music, then!"

'But I was mistaken. I did not then know that *primo piano* simply meant the first-floor of the house. All the brigands, excepting two, went upstairs. These two remained to guard me, after requesting me to take a seat in the chimney corner. One of them had appropriated my gun, the other my game-bag. As for my hundred crowns and my ring, they had become quite invisible.

'A few moments later there was a call from upstairs. I did not understand what was said, but, as the men again took me by the collar and pushed me towards the stairs, I concluded that I was wanted on the first floor.

'I was not mistaken, gentlemen. On entering, I saw the Captain seated at a well-served table, with numerous bottles of diverse shapes before him, and a very pretty girl at his side. The Captain was from five and thirty to forty years of age; he was what one might call a really fine-looking man; and he was dressed exactly like a stage brigand, in blue velvet, with a red sash and silver buckles, so that I merely thought myself at a rehearsal and was not at all intimidated, as the man perhaps imagined I should be.

'As for the young person in his company she was dressed like one of the Roman peasant girls in Robert's pictures, which I have since seen, that is in a bodice worked with gold, a short motley skirt and red stockings. Her feet were so small she seemed scarcely to have any. But such was my presence of mind that I immediately noticed my ring on one of her fingers, a circumstance, which, added to the company she was keeping, gave me a very low opinion of her.

'On reaching the threshold of the room my custodians relaxed their grip, but remained waiting at the head of the stairs. I took a few steps forward, and after bowing first to the lady, then to the Captain, and finally to all the assembled company, I waited.

"'Here is the musician you asked for," said the Picard.

'Then, once more, I bowed.

"'To what country do you belong?" the Captain inquired in French but with a strong Italian accent.

"'I am a Frenchman, your Excellency!"

"'Ah! I am very glad to hear it," said the young woman in the purest Parisian. For my part I was delighted to find that everybody spoke French, more or less.

"'And you are a musician?" the Captain resumed.

"'I am fourth 'cello at the Theatre of Marseilles."

"'Really!" the girl exclaimed.

"'Picard! Let this gentleman's instrument be brought to him," the Captain commanded; and turning to the girl he added, "And now, my little Rina, I hope that you won't make any further difficulty about dancing?"

"'I have made none," Rina answered, "but you ought to have known that I could not dance without music."

"'Mademoiselle is quite right, your Excellency," said I, "she certainly could not dance without music."

'At that moment, however, one of the brigands appeared at the door, and as much by his gestures as by his words I understood him to say that no instrument of any kind had been found on me.

"'What! no instrument!" roared the Captain.

"'No, Captain," said the Picard, "I swear to you I did not see the slightest sign of any 'cello or anything else."

"'*Bestia*!" the Captain shouted.

"'Captain," said I, "you must not scold that good fellow. These gentlemen searched my person thoroughly, even my flannel undervest, and so, if my 'cello had been concealed about me, they would have found it. But I did not have it with me."

"'You did not have it?"

"'No, but I beg your Excellency to believe that if I had known your partiality for that instrument I would have brought it – indeed I would have brought two rather than one."

"'Very well," said the Captain. "Let five men start at once for Siena, Volterra, Grossetto or any other place they please. But in any case there must be a 'cello here tomorrow evening – and when it arrives you will dance, will you not, my little Rina?"

"'If I am in the humour, and you are amiable," said the young woman.

"'You little rogue!" the Captain retorted, "you know you can do as you like with me." And thereupon he tried to kiss her.

"'What, before company!" exclaimed Rina. "Pretty manners!"

'This public rebuke gave me a better opinion of the young person. Besides, curiously enough, the more I looked at her the less did she seem to be a stranger to me. And yet, however much I might cudgel my memory, I could not remember having ever been in the sort of company she seemed to keep.

'At last, turning to the Captain, the girl exclaimed, "Why you haven't even asked the poor man if he feels hungry."

'I was deeply touched by this solicitude.

"'Well," said the Captain, "are you hungry?"

"'Upon my word, Captain," I replied, "as you are kind enough to inquire, I will frankly own that I dined very poorly at Scarlino, and that a snack would be extremely welcome."

"'Take a seat at the table, then," said he.

"'Yes, take a seat," said Rina with a charming smile. "You must not stand on ceremony with Tonino, who is a friend, or with me, for I am a compatriot of yours."

"'Ah," said I, "the Captain's name is Tonino! That is very pretty and musical."

"'His real name is Antonio," the girl answered with a laugh. "Tonino is a pet name which I have given him," and looking up into his eyes with an expression which even the Captain's patron saint would have been unable to withstand, she added, "And I call him by it because I am so fond of him."

"'Enchantress!" murmured the Captain.

'Meantime, however, a cover had been set, and a chair placed for me with all possible respect. I began to understand that my position with Captain Tonino might prove more endurable than I had at first imagined, for I should be treated with the consideration due to an artiste. Indeed, Mademoiselle Rina herself now kindly passed me the dishes, and filled my glass with wine, thus enabling me to make quite sure that it was indeed my ring which was sparkling on her finger. From time to time I glanced at her face, and the more I did so, gentlemen, the more positive I felt that I had seen her somewhere previously. As for the Captain, he amused himself by toying with her hair, thereby earning more than one sharp rap on the knuckles. And he constantly repeated, "You will dance, won't you, my little Rina," to which she invariably retorted, "We will see."

'When I had supped, Mademoiselle Rina judiciously remarked that I might be in need of repose. This was true, and indeed, though it is impolite to yawn – I do not say that for you, Monsieur Jadin – I was yawning enough to dislocate my jaw. So without waiting to be told twice that I might go to bed, I asked for my room, retired to it, and slept soundly for fifteen consecutive hours.

'The Captain was waiting impatiently for me to awake, yet he was polite enough not to disturb me, which seemed very delicate behaviour on the part of a brigand chief. But I had scarcely sneezed – I am in the habit of sneezing as I awake – when some men entered my room carrying no fewer than five violoncellos. Each messenger had brought back one, and I could not help remarking that, as a natural consequence, the value of 'cellos would rise in that neighbourhood. My observation made the Captain smile, and when I had selected the best of the five instruments, the other four were broken up for firewood.

'I was requested to repair to the Captain's quarters with the 'cello I had chosen, as they were there waiting dinner for me. You will understand that I did not allow them to wait any longer. There was a large table laid for the Captain, Mademoiselle Rina, the Picard, (who was the Lieutenant of the band) and myself; and seven or eight smaller tables for all the other men. At one end of the room about three-hundred candles were sparkling, providing a delightful illumination, and I guessed that after dinner we should have a ball.

'The repast was very gay, gentlemen. These bandits were really good fellows, and the Captain, in particular, was in the best possible humour, owing no doubt to the extreme graciousness of Mademoiselle Rina. Directly the meal was finished, he turned to her saying, "You know, my little Rina, what you promised me?"

'"But I have not refused, have I?" she answered with a smile. And here let me mention that she really had a captivating smile.

'"Well then, go and get ready, but don't be long," said the Captain.

'"Place your watch on the table," she retorted.

'"There it is."

'"I shall require a quarter of an hour. Is that too much?"

'"No, certainly not," I boldly answered.

'"Well, a quarter of an hour then," said the Captain.

'"Tripping as lightly as any fawn, Mademoiselle Rina quitted the room.

'"Now I hope you mean to distinguish yourself, Master Musician," said the Captain to me.

'"I will do my best," I answered.

"'That's right, and if I am satisfied with you, your hundred crowns shall be returned to you."

"'And my ring, Captain?"

"'Oh! as for your ring, you must bid it goodbye. Besides, as you know, Rina has it, and you are surely too gallant to wish to deprive her of it."

'I believe I pulled a somewhat wry face as I nodded assent, but at all events the Captain appeared to be satisfied.

"'As for you, my men," he resumed, "I am going to give you a treat fit for the College of Cardinals. I hope you will be pleased with it."

"'*Evviva il Capitano!*" replied the brigands.

'At this moment Mademoiselle Rina appeared on the threshold, and with one bound, reached the middle of the room.

'Gentlemen, she was costumed like a bayadère, with a silver bodice, a large cashmere shawl serving as a sash, gauze skirts which scarcely reached her knees, and silk fleshings. She looked charming. I grasped my 'cello, fancying myself at the Theatre of Marseilles again.

"'To what air would you like to dance, Mademoiselle?" I asked her.

"'Do you know the *pas de châle* in the ballet of Clari?" she inquired.

"'Certainly," said I, "it is my favourite."[2]

"'Begin then, I am ready."

'I started on the ritournello. The brigands mustered all around.

'At the very first bars, Mademoiselle Rina bounded like a sylph. Her capers, her jetés, her pirouettes, were all splendid. The brigands shouted, "*Brava! Bravissimia!*" like madmen; and for my part it seemed to me that I knew those limbs, that I had seen them dancing somewhere before, gentlemen. I never forget the style of a dancer whom I have once observed.

'She did not seem to grow tired. Indeed the applause must have stimulated her. She was up, she was down, she leaped, she whirled, and all in the most graceful manner! The Captain seemed to lose his senses, and on my side I felt half mad, for it seemed to me that those legs of hers recognized me as much as I recognized them. I almost believed that if they could have spoken they would have exclaimed familiarly, "How do you do, Monsieur Louet?"

'But in the middle of the dance the inn-keeper entered, looking quite alarmed, and whispered a few words in the Captain's ear.

"'*Ove sono*? Where are they?" the Captain quietly inquired.

"'At San Dalmazio," the inn-keeper replied.

---

[2] It is evident that M. Louet, like Alfred Jingle of Pickwickian fame, was endowed with the gift of anticipation. His adventure befell him in the year 1810, and *Clari, the Maid of Milan*, was not produced till 1822!

"'Well, we will finish the dance, we have plenty of time."

"'What is the matter?" asked Mademoiselle Rina now, as she drew herself up with her arms extended.

"'Nothing, nothing," the Captain answered. "It seems that those rascally travellers, who were stopped yesterday, have given the alarm at Siena and Florence, and that the Grand Duchess Eliza's Hussars are on our track."

"'Well, fortunately I have finished my dance," said Rina with a laugh.

"'Oh! just one more pirouette, my little Rina," the Captain entreated.

"'Well, I won't refuse you. The last eight bars again, Monsieur, if you please – Well?"

"'I am looking for my bow, Mademoiselle," I stammered. Truth to tell, the bow had dropped from my hand when I heard the news about the Hussars. But those same tidings seemed to have imparted fresh strength to Mademoiselle Rina. I should think that she had never before scored such a triumph. However, a last bound brought her to the door by which she had previously quitted the room in order to dress, and then, after curtseying and kissing her hand to the Captain, she left the room.

"'Now to arms!" the Captain cried. "Let a horse be saddled for Rina, and another for the musician. We ourselves will go on foot. And the Romano road, remember! Those who may go astray are to join again at Chianciano, between Chiusa and Pianza."

"'What, Monsieur!" said I to the Captain, "you mean to take me with you?"

"'Of course! How can Rina dance if there is no music? And how can I do without the sight of her dancing?"

"'But you will expose me to a thousand dangers, Captain?"

"'Neither more nor less than ourselves."

"'But it is your profession, Captain, and it is not mine."

"'Well, how much did you earn at your barn of a theatre?"

'That, gentlemen, is how he spoke of the Theatre of Marseilles.

"'I was paid eight-hundred francs, Captain," I answered.

"'Well, I'll pay you a thousand crowns. What manager would give you as much?"

'No reply was possible. I had to make the best of my lot.

"'Everything is ready now," said the Picard, hastily returning.

"'And here am I!" added Rina, running in, attired once more in her peasant costume.

"'Then let us start," said the Captain.

"'The Hussars! The Hussars!" the inn-keeper shouted; whereupon we all ran towards the stairs.

'But the Captain looked round. "Thunder and lightning!" he said to me savagely, "you are forgetting your 'cello!"

'I took up the instrument, gentlemen, desperately wishing that it had been possible for me to hide inside it. On reaching the door, we found the horses ready.

'"Well, Monsieur," said Rina to me, "won't you assist me to mount. You are not gallant!"

'I offered her my arm in a mechanical way, and as I did so she slipped a scrap of paper into my hand. A cold perspiration gathered on my forehead. What could she have written on that paper? Was it a declaration? Had my personal appearance fascinated her? Had I become the Captain's rival? For a moment I felt inclined to throw the paper away, but curiosity prevailed, and I slipped it into my pocket.

'"The Hussars! the Hussars!" called the inn-keeper once more.

'Indeed, a clatter like that of galloping horsemen could be heard coming from the highroad.

'"Mount, you clumsy oaf!" cried the Picard, catching hold of me by the seat of my breeches, and half hoisting me into the saddle. "There, that will do! Now, men, fasten his 'cello on his back."

'I felt them tying the instrument to me. Then a couple of men took Mademoiselle Rina's horse by the bridle, and two others grasped the bridle of mine. The Captain, with a carbine on his shoulder, ran on beside the young woman. The Picard ran beside me. The rest of the band, some eighteen or twenty men, followed behind. But, all at once, five or six shots were fired at us from a distance of some three-hundred paces, and we heard the bullets whistling past.

'"To the left!" the Captain commanded. "To the left!"

'Directly this order was given we diverged from the road, plunging into a kind of valley, through which a mountain stream coursed. I have never before found myself on horseback, and, in order to retain my seat, I was compelled to grasp the animal's mane with one hand, and his tail with the other. It is fortunate, gentlemen, that a horse is so well provided with hair.

'When we were well in the valley, the Captain ordered a halt. We did so, and listened. The Hussars could be heard galloping furiously along the highway.

'"If they keep up that speed," said the Picard, "they will soon reach Grosseto."

'"Let them go!" the Captain answered. "We will follow the stream. The noise we make will be covered by the rush of the water."

'We went on in this fashion for about an hour and a half, then reached a point where another stream joined the one we had been following.

'"Is that not the Orcia?" asked the Captain in an undertone.

'"No, no," the Picard replied. "That's only the Orbia. The Orcia is at least four miles lower down."

'We resumed our journey, and an hour later we found a second stream flowing into ours, for our line of march had been along a river bed. So you see, Monsieur Méry, the Var is not the only river which cries out for water.

"'Ah! I know where we are now," said the Captain. "To the left! To the left!"

'The order was immediately obeyed. At last, about four o'clock in the morning, we reached a highway.

"'Come, keep up your courage," the Picard said to me, on hearing my moans, for I felt extremely sore. "Here is the highroad to Siena. In another hour and a half we shall reach Chianciano."

'As you may suppose, we merely crossed the highroad, for frequented spots were not to the liking of the brigands. When we had gone another thousand yards or so, we came to some mountains; and briefly, as the Picard had prophesied, in another hour and a half, at about daybreak, we reached Chianciano. The inn-keeper there received us as if we were expected. It seemed as though they were regular customers of his.

'We have been travelling for twelve hours, and, according to my calculations, we had covered as much as twenty leagues of country. When I was lifted from my horse, with the 'cello, I felt as stiff as the instrument itself. So, while the brigands asked for breakfast, I asked for a bed.

'They led me into a little room whose only window was barred, while the door opened into the room where the men took their meal. There could be no thought of escaping. Besides, even if I had been minded to try, I was physically incapable of any effort.

'As I undressed I suddenly remembered the paper which Mademoiselle Rina had handed me, and which I had forgotten during our nocturnal journey. Even if I had remembered it, however, I could not have read it, on account of the darkness. But at first light I took a look at it.

'It was a little note, written in pencil, and beginning in this fashion, "My dear Monsieur Louet." When I saw these words, much as I desired to read the rest, I paused in astonishment. "Dear me!" I thought, "so Mademoiselle Rina knows my name."

'Then I continued reading as follows,

As you may suppose, the company in which we find ourselves is no more to my liking than it is to yours, but to give it the slip prudence is even more necessary than courage. When the proper time comes I trust that you will be deficient in neither. Besides, I shall set you an example. Meantime, pretend you don't know me.

I wish I could have returned you your ring, for I have noticed how anxiously you have glanced at it, but I must keep it, for I need it to effect our joint deliverance. For the present, farewell, Monsieur Louet. We shall meet again some day, I hope – you in the orchestra of the Theatre of Marseilles and I on the stage there.

Zéphirine

P.S. Swallow this note.

★　★　★

'The signature explained everything, gentlemen! Mademoiselle Rina was none other than little Zéphirine, who by reason of her prodigious success had been re-engaged three years running at the Theatre of Marseilles. You cannot remember her, Monsieur Méry, you are too young. But you see by this how people meet again.

'I read the note a second time and was then particularly struck by the postscript, "Swallow this note." It was a prudent course to take, though by no means a pleasant one. However, I decided to do as Mademoiselle Zéphirine desired, and went to sleep, feeling more at ease now that I knew I had a friend in the company.

'I was slumbering soundly, when all at once somebody shook my right arm. I sneezed – I have already admitted, I think, that I always sneeze when I awake – and as I opened my eyes I saw it was the Picard, the Lieutenant of the band, who had ventured to rouse me in this unceremonious manner.

'"Up! up!" he called. "The Hussars are at Monte Pulciano. We must start in a quarter of an hour."

'I made one leap from my bed to my clothes. The bullets of the previous evening were still whistling unpleasantly in my ears.

'The first person I saw on quitting my room was Mademoiselle Zéphirine, who seemed as gay as a lark. I admired her strength of mind, and resolved to imitate it. As a first step, in order to reassure her, I signed to her with my finger that I had swallowed her note. She doubtless thought that if this were all I had swallowed since our arrival at the inn, I must be in need of additional sustenance, for turning to the Captain, with a laugh, she said, "Tonino, our musician is making signs that he is as empty as his instrument. Is there not time for him to eat something before we start?"

'"Pooh! pooh!" replied the Captain, "he can have something at Sorano."

'"Are they all ready, then?" asked Zéphirine.

'"Wait a moment, I will see," said Tonino; and, leaving the room, he called to his men, "Are you ready?"

'While he was gone Zéphirine ran to the window, drew my ring from her finger, and swiftly scratched something on the glass. When the Captain returned he found her standing where he had left her.

"'Come, come," said he, "we shall have time to rest at Sorano." And he added between his teeth, "Either we have been betrayed, or those devilish Hussars are sorcerers!"

'Then, bidding me go ahead, he gave his arm to Zéphirine, and we went downstairs. The horses were ready as on the previous night. Similar arrangements were made, and we travelled in a similar manner. Only, as we started during the daytime, we reached our destination earlier. All the same, we found there was scarcely anything to eat at the wretched inn to which the Captain conducted us, and if Mademoiselle Zéphirine had not generously shared her supper with me I should have gone to bed hungry.

'I had not been lying down more than ten minutes when I heard a most terrible racket. Jumping out of bed I caught hold of my clothes, opened the door and asked, "Whatever is the matter?"

'The bandits, armed to the teeth, swarmed round me.

"'The matter is that we are surrounded by those cursed Hussars." cried the Lieutenant. "There must be some traitor among us. If I thought it was you——"

'But at that moment the inn-keeper opened a door conducting to a private staircase, and called, "This way! This way!"

'The Captain at once sprang down the stairs, holding Mademoiselle Zéphirine by the hand. The Picard pushed me next, and the rest of the band followed.

'At the foot of the stairs the inn-keeper entered a little wood-house, went to a trap door in one corner and raised it. Not another word was spoken, but the Captain understood everything. He went down through the trap by a ladder, at the same time assisting Mademoiselle Zéphirine to descend. We all followed, and heard the inn-keeper shutting the door above us and covering it with faggots, while the Picard for his part removed the ladder. Thus, those who might wish to join us in our retreat would have to jump one by one, a height of about fifteen feet.

'I need hardly tell you that I immediately profited by this respite to dress myself.

'A few moments elapsed, and then we heard a terrific banging at the inn door, as if somebody were trying to beat it in.

"'*I schioppi sono caricati*?"[3] asked the Captain.

'As this was much the same question that the coach-driver had asked me respecting my gun, I understood it. Besides I heard a sound of ramrods in such of the brigands' firearms as were not yet ready.

"'Gentlemen!" I then exclaimed, "gentlemen, I certainly hope——"

"'Silence, if you wish to go on living." the Picard retorted.

[3] "Are the guns loaded?"

"'Certainly I wish to go on living——" I answered.

"'Shut your mouth then, or I'll gag you!'"

'As I did not desire to be gagged, I said no more, but sought a corner in which I might find some shelter from the impending bullets. Unfortunately there was no such corner in that horrid cavern; it was a veritable dungeon.

'However, we heard the door of the hostelry open; and by the rapping of heels and gun-stocks overhead, we understood that a party of soldiers had entered the house. As you will perceive, we had been followed very closely. There were twenty of us in that cavern, and yet so deep was the silence there that one might have heard the buzzing of a fly. But, up above, matters were very different. It seemed as if the inn were being sacked. The shouts, the imprecations, were enough to make one shudder! Two or three times we heard the soldiers entering the wood-house in which the trap door was located; and our silence was then broken by the cocking of our guns. It was a very faint sound, gentlemen, but it went straight to my heart.

'At last, after the expiration of an hour or so, the noise slowly abated. Perfect stillness ensued, then we heard the faggots being removed, and the trap door was opened. Our host had come to tell us that the Frenchmen,[4] weary of their fruitless search, had departed, and that we might now come out of our hiding place.

'While the brigands drew near to the trap to converse with the inn-keeper, Mademoiselle Zéphirine, who had remained alone with your humble servant at the far end of the cavern, came close and took my hand, saying, "We are saved!"

"'How so?" I inquired.

"'Why, Ernest is on our track."

"'Who is Ernest?"

"'A young officer of Hussars – my lover."

"'Oh, indeed! In that case I know Monsieur Ernest."

"'You know him! A handsome young man of five or six and twenty, about your height, but well made?"

"'The same! I travelled with him from Piombino to—— But stop! I remember now, he spoke to me of you!"

"'He spoke to you of me! Dear Ernest!"

"'But he must be a perfect sorcerer to follow our track so closely."

"'No, my dear Monsieur Louet, he is no sorcerer; but at every inn we reach I write my name on a window-pane, together with that of the next village where we intend to stop."

---

[4] The Hussars were French, the time of the story being the Napoleonic period in Italy.

"'Oh, I understand now! And that is why you require my ring. A thousand apologies, Mademoiselle, for the unworthy suspicions I had formed! The stone must scratch the glass well, for it is a real diamond——"

"'Hush, they are saying something important!"

'Then, for a moment she remained silent, listening to the brigands, whom I myself did not understand, for they were speaking in Italian.

"'Ah! I have it," she exclaimed at last. "Caprarola. Ca-pra-ro-la, remember that name in case I should forget it. It is there we are going——"

"'What!" I exclaimed in alarm, "we are moving on again——"

"'Eh?" said the Picard, suddenly turning round.

"'Nothing, Lieutenant, nothing," I replied. "I was only anxious about my 'cello."

'Zéphirine quickly left me, slipping among the brigands, so that when the Captain looked for her, he found her beside him.

"'Well, my little Rina," said he, "those French devils are gone."

"'I breathe again," she answered. "Which way did they go?"

"'Our host thinks that as they belong to the Grand Duchess's Hussars they have no right to come farther south; but it seems that a young officer, who is with them, has a commission to keep up the pursuit and call out troops wherever he finds any."

"'Then what are we going to do?"

"'Resume our journey."

"'In broad daylight?"

"'Oh! have no fears, we have roads of our own."

"'But I am really very tired."

"'Come, show a little courage, Rina. We haven't much farther to go – thirty-five miles at the utmost. By tomorrow night we shall be in safety."

"'Then let us start."

"'Forward!" said the Captain.

"'But what about my 'cello?" I asked the Picard.

"'Oh! don't be uneasy. It has not been harmed."

"'Good!" said I; for as you will understand, gentlemen, that 'cello was my safeguard.

'Well, we resumed our journey. The inn-keeper acted as our guide, and did not quit us till we had reached what the Captain called one of his own roads. It was truly one of Satan's!

'About noon we entered a large forest, a perfect brigands' forest, and I am sure that we should have met with some unpleasant encounter if we had not been in such good company. About four o'clock we reached Caprarola, where we at last spent a quiet day and night, undisturbed by Monsieur Ernest, who had hitherto prevented us from either eating or sleeping. For the moment he had either lost our track or else lacked sufficient forces to pursue us. The inn was badly provisioned, but a messenger was sent to the nearest town, Ronciglione, I think, and returned with enough supplies for a fairly good dinner.

'At three in the morning we were awakened but as I had retired to rest at six in the evening, I had managed to get from eight to nine hours sleep. That is what I require, gentlemen. If I do not get a full eight hours, I feel quite wretched.

'This time the journey was a short one. About eleven in the morning, we were ferried across a river, then halted for lunch at an inn which was called, I heard, the Osteria Barberina.

'"Ah!" said the Captain, "now we are at home."

'"What! at home in this wretched inn!" replied Zéphirine, pouting. "Why, where is the wonderful castello you talked to me about?"

'"Oh! I only mean that we are now on our own estates, and that from this point onwards you may command as freely as any queen."

'"Then my commands are that you place this room at my disposal for a few minutes, for I don't wish to show myself to my subjects of—— What is the name of our castle?"

'"Anticoli."

'"Well, to my subjects of Anticoli, in my present travel-stained condition. Why, I look a perfect fright!"

'"*Civetta*! You coquette!" said the Captain smiling.

'"Go, go! I shall be ready in a quarter of an hour." And thereupon, Zéphirine put us out of the room and locked herself inside it.

'"So you have a castle, Captain?" said I.

'"Something of the kind," he answered.

'"Is it your own property?"

'"Oh, no! In that case I might be troubled by the Government. It belongs to a Roman nobleman who lends it me. I pay him a small rent. The honest man is kept in the city by the duties of his office, and of course he must turn his country-place to some use."

'"Then we shall be as happy there as fighting cocks?"

'"Precisely! We may have to do a little fighting now and then, but that is one of the pleasures of our profession."

'"Oh, I did not mean that!" I stammered. "I must remind you, Captain, that I am only in your service as a 'cellist."

'"But what about that gun and game-bag you claimed as your own?"

'"They were certainly mine – and, by the way, is there any good shooting on the estate you speak of Captain?"

'"Splendid shooting!"

'"What sort of game is there, then?"

'"All sorts."

"'Any *chastres*?"

"'*Chastres*, indeed! Yes, flocks of them!"

"'That's capital, Captain." said I. "Then I'll keep the table supplied with game."

"'All right. I will lend you three or four of my men to beat the cover, and you shall have as much shooting as you desire."

"'You were always good enough to promise me——'"

"'What?'"

"'My hundred crowns.'"

"'That's true. Picard, see that those hundred crowns are returned to this gentleman."

"'Really, Captain," said I, "it is strange that anybody should wish you harm. You are the most honest brigand I ever met."

'At this moment Zéphirine came out of the room. "Here I am," she said.

"'What, already!" the Captain exclaimed.

"'Oh! I can be quick when I like," she answered. "I have had time to do all I needed to."

"'Bravo! In that case we will set off again."

"'I am ready," said Zéphirine, who, while the Captain opened the window and called his men together, had time to exchange a glance with me, and point to the ring she wore. I at once understood what she had been doing while she was left alone in the room.

'We started about two o'clock, and at four we reached the bank of another little river. The Captain called the ferryman, addressing him by his name, and the fellow hastened to us like one who recognized the voice that had summoned him. He and the Captain conversed in whispers while we were crossing.

"'Well," asked Mademoiselle Zéphirine with a well-feigned assumption of uneasiness, "is our castle no longer where it was?"

"'Oh yes," said the Captain smiling, "in another quarter of an hour I hope we shall be installed in it."

"'What a blessing!" exclaimed Zéphirine. "We have been wandering about quite long enough!"

'We passed down a magnificent avenue of poplars at the end of which was a gate, that of the grounds of a magnificent villa. The Captain rang, and the porter opened the gate. As soon as he had recognized the Captain he struck the bell in a particular manner, and five or six servants ran up. It seemed as if the Captain's presence had been greatly desired, for there was much rejoicing among all these retainers. He, however, merely treated their demonstrations like marks of respect which were due to him, and to which he was well accustomed.

"'That will do! that will do!" said he. "Walk ahead and light the way."

'The servants obeyed. One of them wished to relieve me of my 'cello, with the best of intentions no doubt; but as it was an excellent instrument I would not entrust it to him. The result was a trifling squabble, which the Picard terminated by giving the man a violent blow with his fist. Thus I remained in possession of the 'cello, which I had determined to take back to France with me should I ever enjoy the happiness of returning.

'We were shown to our respective apartments. The place was a perfect palace, gentlemen, one of the country palaces of the Roman nobility, as the Captain had said. For my part, I was given a room decorated with magnificent frescoes. It is true that the door opened into the main gallery, and that I could neither enter nor leave the room without passing five or six servants, who, at the very first glance seemed to me to be genuine brigands disguised as lackeys.

'You can imagine, gentlemen, to what a condition I had been reduced by my travels, and I was therefore about to ring and request the loan of a few articles of clothing, when a servant came in with a quantity of linen, shoes, stockings, breeches, dress coats and morning coats, from which he invited me to select whatever might fit me or take my fancy. But I shuddered when I thought that all this apparel must be stolen property; and on that account I contented myself with a riding coat, a dress coat, two pairs of breeches, and six shirts. Nobody could have shown greater moderation under such circumstances.

'Before the servant withdrew he opened the doors of a small bathroom, and told me that dinner would be served *alle vingti-due*. After numerous explanations I gathered that this meant we should dine between six and seven o'clock. I have never been able to understand, however, what *vingti-due*, otherwise twenty-two, had to do with that hour.

'As will be perceived, I had only just enough time for my toilet. Fortunately, I found everything necessary laid out for me on a table, including even some excellent English razors, which I have ever since regretted, for I have never found any equal to them in France.

'Just as I had finished dressing the dinner-bell rang. I gave a final touch to my hair, and quitting the room locked the door and put the key in my pocket fearing that anybody should touch my 'cello in my absence. A servant conducted me to the drawing-room, where a young nobleman, a young lady, and a French officer were already assembled.

'I thereupon thought I must have entered the wrong room, and was about to withdraw, but just was I stepping backwards and I trod on the servant's toes, I heard the young lady say, "Why, what are you about, Monsieur Louet? Don't you intend to dine with us?"

'"I beg your pardon, Mademoiselle," I answered, "but I did not recognize you."

"'If you prefer it, my dear Monsieur Louet," now said the young nobleman, "you may have your dinner served in your own room."

"'Why, Captain, is it you?" I exclaimed. Really gentlemen, I was lost in astonishment.

"'Oh, Monsieur Louet would not be so unkind as to deprive us of his company," remarked the officer who saluted me with a bow.

'I turned to acknowledge his politeness – Gentlemen, it was the Lieutenant. There had been as complete a transformation as in *Cinderella*.

"'*Al suo commodo*," said a footman as he threw back the folding-doors of the dining room.

"'What may that mean, if it is not indiscreet to ask?" I said to the Lieutenant.

"'It means, my dear Monsieur Louet," he replied, "that the soup is on the table."

'The Captain gave his hand to Mademoiselle Zéphirine, and the Lieutenant and I followed them into the well-lighted dining room, where the meal was served in admirable style.

"'I don't know whether you will be satisfied with my cook, Monsieur Louet," said the Captain, taking his place, and showing me mine, "but he is French, and so said to be fairly skilful. I have ordered two or three Provençal dishes expressly for you."

"'What! flavoured with garlic? Fie!" said the Lieutenant, opening a gold snuff box and taking a pinch of perfumed rapee.

'Gentlemen, I thought I was dreaming, particularly when some soup was served me. "Why, this is a bouillabaisse!" said I. And so it was, and an excellent one too.

"'Have you glanced at the park, Monsieur Louet?" the Captain inquired.

"'Yes, your Excellency," I replied, "from the window of my room."

"'It is said to be well-stocked with game," the Captain continued. "You must inspect it tomorrow. You promised to supply us with game, you know."

"'And I renew my promise, Captain." I answered. "Only I must beg you to let me have my own gun. I am accustomed to it, and, somehow, I can never shoot properly with any other."

"'Agreed!" said the Captain.

"'By the bye," Zéphirine now observed, "you know we are to dine early tomorrow, Tonino. You promised to take me to the Teatro della Valle. I am anxious to see the third-rate little dancer who has replaced me there."

"'But there is no performance tomorrow," the Captain answered. "There will be none till the next day. Besides, I do not know whether the carriage is in good order. But I will see to everything, depend on me. Meantime, would you like to ride to Tivoli or Subiaco tomorrow?"

"'Will you join us, Monsieur Louet?" the young woman inquired.

"'No, thank you," I replied, "I am not accustomed to horses, so it would be no pleasure for me to go riding. So, if the Captain has no objections, I will try my luck in the covert. I am a sportsman before anything else."

"'As you please, Monsieur Louet," the Captain replied. "You are free to do as you like."

"'I will keep Monsieur Louet company and shoot with him," said the Lieutenant.

"'I shall feel deeply honoured by your society, Monsieur," I answered, bowing.

'So it was agreed that the Captain and Zéphirine should ride over to Subiaco, while the Lieutenant and myself enjoyed some shooting in the park.

'After dinner I was left at liberty to do as I pleased, and as I had been leading a very trying and restless life for the last fortnight or three weeks, I availed myself of this latitude to return to my room. Picture my astonishment when, on opening the door which I had previously locked, I perceived my gun standing in one corner, my game-bag hanging in another, and my hundred crowns lying on the mantelpiece. From this it was evident that Captain Tonino's servants required no keys to unlock the doors of his villa.

'While I was undressing, the cook, to whom I had sent a complimentary message respecting the bouillabaisse, came to ask me whether I should like to breakfast the next morning in the Provençal, French or Italian style, for, said he, as I intended to go shooting, the Count of Villaforte had given orders that I should be served in my room. From this speech it appeared that Captain Tonino, besides changing his attire, had also thought fit to change his name. But I said nothing of this to the cook. I merely renewed my compliments, and asked him to let me have a chicken fried in oil, commonly called a *poulet à la Provençale*, that, gentlemen, being my favourite dish.

'I spent a very good night, sleeping so soundly that I did not awake till my breakfast arrived at the door. And I breakfasted, gentlemen, like a king. Just as I was draining a cup of chocolate, I felt a tap on the shoulder. I turned, and saw the Lieutenant in a handsome shooting costume.

"'Why!" said he, "are you not ready?"

'I made a thousand apologies to him, but observed, by way of excuse, that I could hardly go shooting in short breeches, whereupon he pointed to a shooting costume similar to his own, which was lying in readiness on a sofa. I was like Aladdin, gentlemen. I merely had to express a wish in order to see it gratified!

'In a few minutes I was ready, and we went downstairs. Outside the house, I saw some servants holding four saddle-horses, one for the Captain, one for Mademoiselle Zéphirine, and two for the grooms who were to accompany them. At the same moment the Captain appeared. He slipped a brace of double-barrelled pistols into his holsters, and the grooms who were to accompany him did likewise. He and they, moreover, wore a kind of fancy dress, which allowed them to carry hunting knives.

'The Captain remarked that I noticed these precautions. "What else can I do, Monsieur Louet?" said he. "There is such a bad police service in this part of the world that you can never be sure of your safety. So as you will understand, it is as well to be armed."

'As a matter of fact I did not understand at all. I had either been dreaming, or else I was dreaming now. Which was illusion, which reality, Captain Tonino, or the Count of Villaforte? That was a point which I could not possibly determine, so I decided to let things take their course.

'And then Mademoiselle Zéphirine appeared, looking quite charming in her riding habit.

'"Well, good luck, Monsieur Louet," said the Captain as he leapt into the saddle. "We shall be back by four o'clock, and I hope your shooting will then be over."

'"I hope so, too, Monsieur le Comte," said I, "but I no longer dare to express an opinion on such matters. There is no telling where a shooting excursion may lead one to."

'"At any rate," continued the Captain, while spurring his horse and making it caracole, "at any rate, Beaumanoir, I leave Monsieur Louet to your care."

'"Be easy, Count," the Lieutenant answered.

'Then, after waving farewell, the Captain and Mademoiselle Zéphirine set off at a canter, followed by the grooms.

'"Excuse me, Monsieur," said I, approaching the Lieutenant, "it was you I believe whom the Count addressed by the name of Beaumanoir?"

'"Quite so."

'"But I thought the Beaumanoir family was extinct?"

'"Well, I have revived it, that's all."

'"You are at liberty to do so, Monsieur," I said. "Allow me to apologize if I was indiscreet."

'"Oh! you need make no excuse, my dear Louet. Would you like a dog or not?"

'"I prefer to have none," I answered. "The last time I went shooting with one, it insulted me abominably, and I should not like the same thing to occur again."

'"As you please. Gaetano, release Romeo for me."

'The shooting began. With my first six shots, gentlemen, I winged four *chastres*, which clearly proved to me that the one I had followed from Marseilles was a bewitched one.

'But Monsieur de Beaumanoir laughed when he noticed what I fired at. "How do you find any amusement in shooting such game as that?" he asked.

'"Indeed, I do, Monsieur," I answered. "At Marseilles the *chastre* is a very rare bird. I never saw but one there in all my life – an extraordinary bird it was, Monsieur; in fact I am indebted to it for the pleasure of now being in your company!"

'"Pooh! You had better reserve your fire for the pheasants, hares and roes."

'"What! are there any such animals here, Monsieur?" I cried in amazement.

'"Look!" cried the Lieutenant. "There is one close to you now!" Indeed, at that very moment a young roebuck bounded past me at a distance of no more than a dozen paces.

'As we advanced, I perceived every now and then various gardeners whom I seemed to have seen somewhere before, gamekeepers, also, whose faces were not unknown to me. They all bowed, gentlemen; yet it occurred to me that they were merely my former brigand companions in different attire. But I had seen so many marvels that I was resolved to let nothing puzzle my brain in future.

'We fired in turn. The park was of great extent, and walled in, with here and there a little stretch of iron railing to allow a view of the surrounding scenery, which was magnificent. I was near some of these railings when Monsieur de Beaumanoir fired at a pheasant.

'At this moment a young countryman, who was looking through the railings, said to me, "*Signore, questo castello, il castello d'Anticoli?*"

'"Excuse me, my good man," I answered, approaching him. "I do not understand Italian. Speak to me in French, and I shall be pleased to answer you."

'"What, is it you, Monsieur Louet?" this seeming peasant then exclaimed.

'"Yes, it is me, but how do you know me?" I inquired.

'"Why, don't you remember me?"

'"Unfortunately, no."

'"You don't remember the Hussar officer, your travelling companion?"

'"Why, is it you, Monsieur Ernest?" I exclaimed, "How delighted Mademoiselle Zéphirine will be!"

'"Is she really here?"

'"Certainly she is, Monsieur Ernest. She is a prisoner like myself."

'"Then Captain Tonino——"

'"Is the Count of Villaforte——"

"'And this property——"

"'A den of brigands, Monsieur!'"

"'That is all I wished to know! Goodbye, Monsieur Louet. If we should be seen chatting together suspicions might be aroused. Tell Zéphirine that she will hear from me tomorrow.'"

'Thereupon he bounded into the forest.

"'Bring it, Romeo, bring it!' Monsieur de Beaumanoir was calling.

'I ran towards him. "Ah! you have brought it down," said I, "a fine cock-pheasant, Monsieur, an extremely fine bird."

"'Yes, yes! But who was that speaking to you, Monsieur Louet?'"

"'A peasant who asked me a question in Italian and to whom I replied that unfortunately I did not understand the language.'"

"'Indeed!' said Monsieur de Beaumanoir in a tone expressive of considerable doubt, accompanied by a distrustful glance. And after reloading his gun, he added, "I think, Monsieur Louet, that as I speak Italian it will be best for me to keep on the side nearest to the wall. In that way, as there may be other peasants desirous of asking you questions, I will undertake to answer them."

"'As you please, Monsieur de Beaumanoir," I replied, "You are in charge here."

'I then immediately changed places with him. But he looked in vain, gentlemen, for he saw nobody.

★   ★   ★

'We had some superb sport. True, Monsieur de Beaumanoir was an excellent shot. At last, at four o'clock, we walked back to the house, and then, as the Count of Villaforte and Mademoiselle Zéphirine had not returned from their ride, I retired to my room intending to prepare for dinner.

'However, as I did not need two hours to dress, I took my violoncello, and played a few bars of music. The instrument was indeed an excellent one, and I quite made up my mind that I would not part with it.

'At half-past five I went down to the drawing-room. I was the first there, but the Count of Villaforte and Mademoiselle Zéphirine joined me a moment afterwards.

"'Well, dear Monsieur Louet," said Mademoiselle, "have you enjoyed yourself?"

"'I should be difficult to please if I hadn't, Mademoiselle," I answered, "And you?"

"'Oh! yes, exceedingly. The environs of Anticoli are delightful.'"

"'Captain!' called the Lieutenant, opening the door and popping his head into the room.

"'Who calls me Captain? I am not Captain here, Beaumanoir, I am the Count of Villaforte," said Tonino.

"'Captain,'" the other repeated in spite of this rebuke, "pray come outside for a moment; it is a matter of importance."

"'Excuse me, then," said the Captain to Zéphirine and me, "business you know, comes before everything."

"'Do as you wish, Count, do as you wish," I answered.

'He left the room. I waited till the door was shut, and when I felt certain he could not hear me, I said to Mademoiselle Zéphirine, "I have seen Monsieur Ernest."

"'When?"

"'Today."

"'Indeed! Ah! the dear fellow, he must have followed us from inn to inn!"

"'Probably, unless he is a sorcerer."

"'And did he not give you a message for me?"

"'He said you would hear from him tomorrow."

"'Oh! how pleased I am! He will deliver us, Monsieur Louet!"

"'But, Mademoiselle," said I, "how does it happen that you keep such company when you despise it so much?"

"'Why," she retorted, "how does it happen that you yourself share it?"

"'I was led into it by force."

"'And do you think, then, that I came willingly? No indeed! Tonino saw me dance at the Theatre of Bologna, fell in love with me, and carried me off!"

"'Good heavens! Then this man has no more respect for dancers than for musicians!"

"'But what worries me most is that Ernest may have thought I had run away with a Cardinal, for there was a Cardinal courting me at the time!"

"'Oh!"

"'Silence! – Tonino is coming back!"

"'Well? well? What is the matter!" Zéphirine exclaimed as she ran towards the Captain. "Oh! how dreadfully upset you look! Is the news very bad, then?"

"'At least it is not good," said he.

"'Has it come from a reliable source?" asked Zéphirine again, with an anxiety which was now far from being feigned.

"'From the best of all sources – from a friend who is in the police service."

"'Good heavens! What do you fear then?"

"'Nothing positive, but something is being plotted against us. We were tracked from Chianciano as far as the Osteria Barberini. They only lost our track behind Monte Gennaro. So, my dear girl, I fear we must defer our projected visit to the Teatro della Valle tomorrow evening."

"'But that won't prevent us from dining, will it, Captain?"

"'Here comes the answer,' he replied.

"'His Excellency, dinner is served,' at that moment exclaimed a footman, opening the door.

'On entering the dining room I perceived a brace of pistols lying beside the Captain's plate, and another pair beside the Lieutenant's. Moreover, each time the door was opened by the footmen who served us, I espied two bandits in the hall, each carrying a carbine. Under these circumstances, our repast, as you may suppose, was a silent one, and though no mishap occurred, I felt instinctively that a catastrophe was approaching, and I could not think of it without feeling some anxiety.

'The meal over, the Captain placed sentries in various parts.

"'My little Rina,' said he, "I must apologize for not keeping you company this evening, but I have to watch over our safety. By and by, instead of going to bed, you would do well to lie down with your clothes on, for we may be disturbed during the night, and I should like you to be quite ready so that I may take you to a place of safety."

"'I will do whatever you wish,' Mademoiselle Zéphirine replied.

"'And I shall be obliged if you, Monsieur Louet, will take the same precautions."

"'I am at your orders, Monsieur le Comte."

"'Now, my little Zéphirine,' he resumed, "I should like you to leave us in possession of the ground floor, for we have a few arrangements to make, at which a lady's presence is not desirable."

"'I will go up to my room,' said Mademoiselle Zéphirine.

"'And I as well,' I added.

'The Captain turned away to ring a bell.

"'Things are progressing well, Monsieur Louet,' Zéphirine whispered to me, rubbing her hands all the while.

"'They are progressing badly, Mademoiselle Zéphirine,' I responded, shaking my head.

"'Conduct this lady and gentleman to their rooms,' said the Captain in Italian to the man who answered his summons. And he added something which we could not hear.

"'I hope all this is merely a false alarm,' said Mademoiselle Zéphirine, as she rose to go.

"'Hm! I don't know why, but I have presentiments,' the Captain answered. "Goodnight – goodnight, Monsieur Louet."

"'Goodnight, Captain,' I responded as I quitted the room.

'Mademoiselle Zéphirine had remained a little in the rear; when I had climbed a dozen steps of the staircase she suddenly disappeared. I wished to wait for her, but the brigand who escorted me, pushed me on by the shoulders.

'I entered my room, the man left me the lamp he was carrying, and then, as he went off, locked my door behind him.

'"Dear me!" I thought, "it seems I am a prisoner."

'My only course was to lie down, and that was what I did. I spent several hours absorbed in melancholy thoughts, but by degrees my mind became confused. From time to time, thinking that I heard some suspicious noise, I gave a start, opened my eyes, and listened. But eventually my sleepiness mastered me, and I dozed off.

'I cannot tell how long I had slept, when a man entered my room and shook me. "*Subito, subito!* – quick, quick!" he called.

'"Is anything the matter, Monsieur?" I asked, sitting up on the bed.

'"*Non, c'è niente, ma bisogna seguir mi.*" – "No, it is nothing, but you must follow me."

'I gathered that the man was telling me to follow him, for I had often heard the word *seguir* during my intercourse with the brigands.

'"But where am I to *seguir* you?" I asked him.

'"*Non capisco – Avanti, avanti!*" – "I don't understand – Forward, forward!"

'"Excuse me," said I, "but I won't leave my 'cello here. I do not wish any harm to happen to my instrument. I hope I am not forbidden to take it."

'The brigand let me understand that I might do so, but that I must make haste. Accordingly, I hoisted the 'cello on my back and followed him. He led me along several passages and then down a small staircase, at the foot of which he opened a door. We then found ourselves in the grounds. The dawn was just breaking.

'I cannot tell you, gentlemen, how many turns and twists we made as we crossed the park. At last we plunged into a maze of trees, in the darkest part of which we saw the entrance of a grotto.

'I understood that this was to be my abode for the present, and I was groping hither and thither, trying to take my bearing, when somebody's hand caught hold of mine. I was about to raise a cry but I remarked that the hand I felt was very smooth, and could not, therefore, be a brigand's.

'"Hush!" said a soft voice.

'"I won't breathe a word, Mademoiselle," I answered.

'"Put your 'cello over there."

'I obeyed and then inquired, "Well, what has happened?"

'"We are surrounded by a regiment, and Ernest commands it!"

'"Ah! the brave fellow!"

'"You see how much he loves me! He has followed us all the way from Siena. What a blessing it is that you were taken prisoner, Monsieur Louet!"

"'Yes, a great blessing!" I answered ironically.

"'And it was my own idea, too."

"'What! Yours?"

"'Yes, certainly. I said I could not dance without a musician, and they kept on seeking one until, at last, they found you."

"'So, it is to you that I am indebted——"

"'Yes, to me, my dear Monsieur Louet, to me – besides which, by means of your ring, I was able to inform Ernest of our travelling plans."

"'But why have we been consigned to this grotto?"

"'Because it is the most secluded spot in the park, and the last where the soldiers are likely to look for us. Besides, there's a door yonder, which probably leads to some vault, and a passage into the fields."

"'But in that case, would it not be best for us to open the door and escape that way, Mademoiselle?"

"'Yes, it would, but unfortunately the door is locked."

'Just then we heard the report of a firearm. "Listen!" I exclaimed.

"'Good! it is beginning," said Zéphirine.

"'Dear me! Where can we hide?" I stammered.

"'Well, I hardly think we can be better hidden than here."

"'At least, Mademoiselle Zéphirine," said I, "you will not forsake me?"

"'Forsake a friend? Never! But on one condition, mind. Ah! listen!"

'The fusillade was becoming louder; it seemed as if the soldiers were firing in volleys.

"'What condition, Mademoiselle?" I faltered. "I will do anything you please."

"'Well, if Ernest should question you about that rascally Captain, you must tell him the strict truth, that I turned my back on the monster all the time, and never gave him the slightest encouragement."

"'But – but will he believe it, Mademoiselle?"

"'What a simpleton you are, Monsieur Louet! He will believe whatever I choose. Haven't I told you that he is in love with me?"

"'Mademoiselle," I said, taking hold of her hand, "the firing seems to increase——"

"'So much the better!" she cried. Ah, gentlemen, that young woman was a very lioness!

'I myself felt emboldened, and to get some idea of what was going on, I went towards the mouth of the grotto.

"'*Dietro, dietro*!" then cried two brigands who were stationed there; and I understood by their imperative gestures that I was to keep back. So I hurriedly did so.

'Meanwhile, things became warmer and warmer every minute. Ah! gentlemen, it was decreed that I should participate in battle – yes, both battles at sea and battles on land!

"'The firing seems to be coming nearer," said Mademoiselle Zéphirine at last.

"'I am afraid so, Mademoiselle," I answered.

"'But on the contrary, you ought to be delighted!" she exclaimed. "It means that the brigands are retreating."

"'I am delighted, Mademoiselle, but I wish they would not retreat this way."

'Shrieks were now heard as if men were being butchered, and in fact so they were, as we saw for ourselves a little later. And amid all those cries arose the rattle of musketry, the blaring of bugles, the beating of drums. The very smell of the powder reached us. And the reports came nearer and nearer, till at last it seemed to me that the combatants were not more than a hundred paces from the grotto.

'Suddenly we heard a sigh; then the heavy thud of a falling body, and one of our two guards rolled into the grotto, struggling convulsively. He had been hit by a random bullet, and as a ray of light reached that part of the grotto where he lay, we could not help witnessing him in the throes of death. But I must acknowledge that at this sight Mademoiselle Zéphirine, so brave only a moment previously, caught hold of my hands, and trembled.

"'Oh! Monsieur Louet," she said, "how dreadful it is to see a man die!"

'But, at that same moment we heard a voice calling, "Stop, scoundrel, stop! Wait for me!"

"'Ernest," cried Mademoiselle Zéphirine. "It is Ernest's voice!" And, with renewed courage, she was darting towards the mouth of the grotto, when the brigand Captain, covered with blood, plunged into it.

"'Zéphirine!" he called wildly, "Zéphirine! Where are you?"

'As he came from the daylight – for the dawn had now risen – he could not at first distinguish us in that dim retreat. Besides, Mademoiselle Zéphirine motioned me neither to stir nor speak. But after the Captain had remained blinded, as it were, for a few moments, his eyes became accustomed to the dimness and searched the depths of the grotto. He then saw us, and sprang forward like a tiger.

"'Why do you not answer when I call you, Zéphirine?" he cried, "Come, come!" And catching her by one arm he tried to drag her to the door at the far end of the cavern.

"'Where are you taking me? Where are you taking me!" cried the poor girl.

"'Come with me, come!"

"'But I don't want to go with you," she answered amid her struggles.

"'What! not go with me!"

"'No, no! Why should I follow you? I don't love you! You carried me off by force; I will not follow you! Ernest! Ernest! Here! here!"

"'Ernest! Ernest!'" gasped the Captain, savagely, "Ah! so it was you who betrayed us!"

"'Monsieur Louet!'" shrieked Zéphirine, "if you are a man, help, quick, save me!"

'Gentlemen, I saw a dagger gleaming! I had no weapon, but I seized my 'cello by the neck, I raised it like a club, and I dealt the Captain such a tremendous blow on the skull that the wood broke, and his head was caught in it. Either the violence of my blow, or his amazement at finding his head imprisoned in a 'cello utterly unnerved the Captain; he flung out his arms and vented such a prodigious roar that the whole grotto shook!

"'Zéphirine! Zéphirine!'" somebody was now calling outside.

"'Ernest! Ernest!'" the young woman answered, bounding towards the entrance.

"'Mademoiselle Zéphirine!'" I, in my turn, shouted as I followed her, quite frightened by my own handiwork.

'I have told you, gentlemen, that this young person was as light as any fawn. She was already in the officer's arms, and I hastened to hide myself behind the loving pair.

"'There! there!'" the young Lieutenant called, showing the mouth of the grotto to a dozen soldiers who had just run up, and who immediately sprang into the cavern. "He is there, bring him out, dead or alive!"

'Five minutes later they reappeared. They had only found the 'cello with the hole which the Captain's head had left in it. He himself had escaped by the farther door.

'But Zéphirine was speaking, "Here, Ernest," said she, "here is my preserver. The dagger was here," and she pointed to her breast, "when he rushed to my help. For I always, always repulsed the monster! And he wanted to kill me to prevent me from joining you!"

"'Really, my love?'" said Ernest.

"'Ah! my dear, can you doubt it? Ask, ask Monsieur Louet!'"

"'Monsieur,'" I said, "I swear to you——"

"'Enough!'" Monsieur Ernest interrupted. "You must not think for a moment that I don't trust her word."

"'I only think, Monsieur Ernest, with all due reference to you, that as the Captain has escaped, the best thing to do now is to place Mademoiselle Zéphirine in safety.'"

"'You are right, Monsieur Louet. Come, Zéphirine.'"

'We walked back to the villa, and in doing so had to cross the battlefield. We saw ten or twelve corpses lying there, and, at the foot of the housesteps, another barred the way.

"'Remove that carcase!'" said a grizzly old corporal, who with two men preceded us.

'The two men turned the body over, and I then recognized the very last of the Beaumanoirs.

'We did not remain long in the villa. Monsieur Ernest left a garrison there, and when Mademoiselle Zéphirine and I had got into the carriage, he, with twelve men armed to the teeth, served as our escort. I need hardly mention, gentlemen, that I had again taken possession of my gun, my game-bag, and my hundred crowns. I only regretted the loss of my poor 'cello, but Mademoiselle Zéphirine apparently regretted nothing whatever. She seemed wild with delight.

'After about an hour's travelling I caught sight of a large city, with a huge dome, on the horizon.

'"If it is not indiscreet on my part, Monsieur Ernest," I said, popping my head out of the carriage window, "may I inquire the name of that city?"

'"The one ahead?"

'"Yes, the one ahead, Monsieur!"

'"Why, that is Rome."

'"Indeed! Rome? Really?"

'"Without any doubt."

'"Well, Monsieur, I am delighted," said I, "upon my word, quite delighted. I have always been most desirous of seeing Rome."

'Two hours later we entered the city. It really was Rome, Monsieur Dumas,' said Monsieur Louet.

'And did you see the Pope also?' I enquired, 'for I remember that was one of your desires.'

'Why, you must know,' replied Monsieur Louet, 'that the worthy old man was then at Fontainebleau.[5] However, I saw him on his return in 1814, him and his successors, for as Monsieur Ernest procured me an engagement as 'cellist at the Teatro della Valle, I remained at Rome till 1830. When at last I returned to Marseilles – I had been away twenty years – at first they wouldn't give me back my place in the orchestra. They regarded me as an imposter, a sort of second Martin Guerre.

'And what became of Mademoiselle Zéphirine?'

'I heard she married Monsieur Ernest, whose surname I never knew, and became a lady of high degree.'

'And did you ever see anything more of the brigand Captain?'

'Indeed I did. Three years later he was recognized and arrested at the same Teatro della Valle, and I had the pleasure of seeing him hanged. And that, messieurs, is how, from one evening having forgotten to discharge my gun, which consequently hung fire when I tried to wing

[5] The Pope in question was Pius VII, who had been carried off by Napoleon I.

a *chastre*, I ended up by visiting Italy and spending twenty years in Rome.'

'Well now, do you know what time it is?' Méry observed at the conclusion of Monsieur Louet's recital, pulling his watch from his fob. 'It is four o'clock in the morning – a pretty time to go to bed!'

'Fortunately,' said Monsieur Louet, pointing to Jadin and the other members of our little party who were already slumbering, 'fortunately those gentlemen have not waited to snatch forty winks!'